COMPENSATION

Rewarding and Retaining Talent

Thomas J. Norman, Ph.D.

CALIFORNIA EDITION

DIRECT TALENT

ATTRACT TALENT

REWARD TALENT

TRANSFORM TALENT

Cover photograph by Aleksander J. Norman

Compensation: Rewarding and Retaining Talent: California Edition

First Edition

This book is intended for educational purposes. Compensation law changes frequently; while every effort has been made to ensure accuracy as of publication, readers should consult current statutes, regulations, and qualified counsel before making compensation decisions. The cases and examples are used for instruction and do not constitute legal or financial advice.

ISBN (PDF): 979-8-9963781-1-1

ISBN (Kindle eBook): 979-8-9963781-0-4

ISBN (Paperback): 979-8-9963781-2-8

ISBN (Hardcover): 979-8-9963781-3-5

Published independently in the United States of America.

Dedication

For Sherri Lynne Norman —

my wife, my rock, and the mother of our three amazing children, Aleksander, Benjamin, and Abigail.

Through every chapter of a winding career — first in management and then in the academy, on opposite coasts and in between — Sherri has been my steadiest source of strength, encouragement, and joy. Her own career experiences have taught me as much as my own have. She agreed to move us from Minnesota to Northern California, back to Minnesota, and at last to Southern California, where I have landed in my first and last academic post at California State University, Dominguez Hills. She was beside me through the long nights of the dissertation and through every transition since.

The best memories sit in the spaces between the work — the rainy campgrounds, the front row of the Royal Shakespeare Company, the time we have made for each other across decades and time zones. Thank you, Sherri, for everything, and for letting me try to keep my old promise of a lifetime of honeymoons.

— Thomas

Preface

Most compensation textbooks treat pay as paperwork — a set of forms, formulas, and compliance boxes to check. I have spent my career, first as a practitioner and then as a professor, convinced that this view gets it backward. Compensation is one of the most strategic levers an organization has: it is how we direct people toward what matters, attract the talent we need, reward the contributions we value, and keep the people who make everything else possible. Done well, a reward system is built into the strategy of the organization; done poorly, it is bolted on afterward and quietly works against everything leaders say they want.

This book grows out of two convictions. The first is that students and managers learn compensation best through real decisions and real numbers, not abstractions. Before I taught this material I designed it — running a global employee-survey program, re-engineering a human resources function, and rebuilding sales compensation at a technology company competing for talent against much larger rivals. That experience taught me that compensation is a tool managers actually have to pick up and use.

The second conviction is that California changes the conversation. With the most demanding pay laws in the country — pay transparency, equal pay, expanded pay-data reporting, agricultural overtime, prevailing wage, and a vast public sector — California makes visible what is true everywhere: a reward system must be designed to be seen and defended in the open. Rather than treat the state as a footnote, this book makes it the running case.

Holding the book together is the DART model — Direction and Deployment, Assessment and Attraction, Rewarding and Retaining, and Teaching and Transforming of talent — a framework I developed to give managers a shared language for connecting pay to performance. Whether you are a student preparing for a career in human resources or public administration, or a manager trying to build a pay system you can stand behind, my hope is that you come to see compensation as I do: not as paperwork, but as one of the most powerful and humane tools we have for building strong organizations.

Thomas J. Norman, Ph.D.
Los Angeles, California

A Note on Sources

The bibliography of this book draws on four distinct kinds of source, and the distinctions matter for how a reader should weigh any particular claim.

The first kind is peer-reviewed scholarship — the academic literature that grounds the theoretical chapters. Vroom's (1964) expectancy theory, Adams's (1965) equity theory, Becker's (1964) human-capital theory, Jensen and Meckling's (1976) agency theory, and Appelbaum and colleagues' (2000) ability–motivation–opportunity framework are foundational sources of this kind. They have survived decades of empirical testing, and the empirical claims this book makes about how pay shapes behavior trace back to them.

The second kind is primary government and regulatory material: California statutes and Labor Code sections, agency guidance from the Department of Industrial Relations and the Civil Rights Department, federal agency rulings, and court opinions. When this book makes a claim about California law, it cites the primary source. Students should always do the same in their own work. California's compensation environment changes often enough that primary-source verification is a discipline rather than a courtesy.

The third kind is practitioner literature — trade books written by executives, consultants, and journalists. Doerr's Measure What Matters, Sinek's Start with Why and The Infinite Game, Brown's Daring Greatly, Rising Strong, and Dare to Lead, Buckingham and Clifton's Now, Discover Your Strengths, Buckingham and Coffman's First, Break All the Rules, Clifton and Harter's It's the Manager, Lafley and Charan's The Game-Changer, Lafley and Martin's Playing to Win, Guidara's Unreasonable Hospitality, and Duckworth's Grit all sit in this category. These sources are valuable for the vocabulary they give students, the frameworks they introduce, and the contemporary practice they describe. They are not substitutes for peer-reviewed evidence, however, and several of them rest on proprietary data sets that have been criticized for methodological opacity. When this book cites them, the citation indicates a framework or a practitioner perspective, not a settled empirical finding. The Clifton and Harter (2019) claim that managers account for roughly seventy percent of the variance in team engagement, for example, is a Gallup finding from a Gallup-published book; the underlying methodology is not openly available for replication. The claim is useful as orientation. It is not a piece of evidence in the same sense as a peer-reviewed meta-analysis.

A subset of the third category deserves a separate note. Some authors of practitioner books also publish in peer-reviewed venues, and the trade book distills that academic work for general readers. Bono and his colleagues, cited in Chapter 9, publish their gratitude research in journals; the trade book Making Grateful Kids (Froh and Bono, 2014) summarizes that work. Duckworth's (2016) Grit draws on the peer-reviewed research she has published as a University of Pennsylvania psychologist. When the book cites these trade titles, the underlying empirical claims rest on the peer-reviewed literature behind them.

The fourth kind is journalism — Fortune, The Wall Street Journal, The Washington Post, NPR, and similar outlets. These sources are cited for recent events such as acquisitions, settlements, contract negotiations, court rulings, and labor actions, where primary-source confirmation either does not yet exist or remains inaccessible. Where possible, the book pairs a journalistic source with the underlying primary document.

Two further notes about how the book uses its sources deserve to be flagged in advance.

The DART model that organizes the book — Direction and Deployment, Assessment and Attraction, Rewarding and Retaining, Teaching and Transforming — is the author's own pedagogical framework, not a peer-reviewed instrument. It is offered as a teaching scaffold that has held up well in the classroom and in consulting practice. Students should engage with it critically: ask whether the four elements are exhaustive, whether the multiplicative form holds up empirically, and whether other organizing frames might fit a specific case better. The model's value is that it forces an integrated view of the reward system. Its limitation is that it is not yet empirically validated in the way that, for example, the AMO framework has been.

The From-the-Field sidebars throughout the book are first-person accounts from the author's own career — at Procter & Gamble, US Bank, and elsewhere. They are presented as personal observation rather than data, and they are used where a story can do pedagogical work that a citation cannot. They are illustration, not evidence. Where they reflect institutional history that students can verify — the P&G compensation tradition, the Wells Fargo cross-selling pattern — the surrounding text cites the documentary sources behind the story.

The discipline this book asks of its students is the discipline this note asks of itself. Whenever a claim matters, ask who made it, what kind of source carries it, what would falsify it, and whose interests the framing serves. Compensation systems decide who gets what. The sources behind a compensation argument deserve at least as much scrutiny as the argument itself.

Contents

Detailed Contents

COMPENSATION: REWARDING AND RETAINING TALENT · CALIFORNIA EDITION

CHAPTER 1

Chapter 1. Why Rewarding Talent Matters

The DART model, the pay model, and the two jobs every paycheck performs.

Thomas J. Norman, Ph.D.

Photograph by Thomas J. Norman

> **OPENING CASE · LOS ANGELES UNIFIED TRIES TO BREAK THE CYCLE**
>
> By 2023, the Los Angeles Unified School District, the second-largest in the nation, faced a familiar and self-reinforcing problem. Persistent vacancies strained the educators who remained, heavier workloads pushed more of them toward the exit, and each departure made the next vacancy harder to fill. The district projected it could lose roughly seven percent of its educators in a single year (LAist, 2023).
>
> The response was telling. The district and United Teachers Los Angeles agreed to raise salaries by about 21 percent through 2025, but the deal did not stop at pay. It also reduced class sizes and committed to hiring more psychologists, social workers, and counselors (ABC7 Los Angeles, 2023). Leaders had concluded that a raise alone would not break the cycle; the reward had to be paired with the right roles, the right staffing, and a workplace people would stay in.
>
> *That insight is where this book begins. Compensation is powerful, yet it works best as one part of a larger system for directing, attracting, rewarding, and transforming talent.*

Learning Objectives

After studying this chapter, you should be able to do the following:

1. Define compensation and total rewards, and explain why pay is best understood as a strategic system rather than an administrative task.
2. Describe the DART model and its four elements: Direction and Deployment, Assessment and Attraction, Rewarding and Retaining, and Teaching and Transforming.
3. Explain the two jobs compensation performs at once: as an incentive and as a sorting mechanism.
4. Apply the pay model, its objectives, policy choices, and techniques, to a real organization.
5. Identify the major forms of pay (cash, benefits, and relational returns) and the main stakeholder perspectives on compensation.
6. Explain how California's pay transparency and equal pay rules, and its immigrant-heavy low-wage workforce, shape reward strategy.

Am I Being Paid What I'm Worth?

Almost every working person eventually wrestles with a deceptively simple question: am I being paid what I am worth? By the end of this book you will see why it is one of the most consequential questions any leader of a public, private, or nonprofit organization ever has to answer. Compensation is often treated as an administrative task, but it is far more useful to view it as a strategic system for directing effort, supporting organizational goals, and shaping employee decisions about whether to join, stay, grow, and perform.

What the question often misses is that the answer depends only partly on the paycheck. Gallup's three decades of engagement research, summarized in Clifton and Harter (2019), trace roughly seventy percent of the variance in team engagement to the immediate manager. The number is striking because it suggests that what most employees experience as a problem with their pay is in part a problem with the relationship that pay travels through. This book takes the finding seriously: compensation is the design layer, coaching is the activation layer, and neither performs the other's job.

It is tempting to assume that paying well is simply a cost that drags an employer down. That assumption is wrong. Google and Nucor Steel both pay generously and remain enormously profitable. The reason is that the demand for labor is a derived demand: a wage exists only when the work produces something an employer, or for government the public, values enough to pay for. Google pays at the very top of the market because its product is software written by elite engineers, and you cannot run Google's business with average talent. Nucor pays its steelworkers more than its competitors do and gets dramatically higher productivity in return, because its incentive system rewards production and quality. Pay alone does not determine outcomes. Attracting talent and getting the most from that talent does.

The opposite strategy carries its own risks. Hyundai and its affiliate Kia built much of their American success on a fast-growing, largely non-union manufacturing footprint across the South, from Alabama to a sprawling new electric-vehicle complex in Georgia. Keeping labor costs low was central to the model, but cost pressure has a way of surfacing downstream. In 2024 the United States Department of Labor sued a Hyundai parts supplier and its staffing agency after investigators found a thirteen-year-old working on an Alabama assembly line that made components for Hyundai vehicles (U.S. Department of Labor, 2024). The following year, federal agents raided a Hyundai battery plant under construction in Georgia and detained roughly 475 workers in what officials called the largest single-site immigration enforcement operation in the agency's history, halting work for months (CNN, 2025). The lesson is not that Hyundai pays too little. It is that compensation strategy reaches far beyond the paycheck, into legal exposure, reputation, and whether the work gets done at all.

Two Jobs at Once: Incentive and Sorting

Compensation does two things at the same time. It is an incentive: it influences what people do once they are on the payroll, including whether they show up, stay, build skills, and perform day in and day out. It is also a sorting mechanism: it shapes who applies, who accepts an offer, and who chooses to remain. These two functions are deeply connected, and they matter as much in public administration as they do in corporate America.

Take the City of Los Angeles trying to hire civil engineers. The city competes for that talent against private firms. If the city's pay scale lags too far behind the market, the sorting problem hits first: strong candidates never apply. The incentive problem follows: the engineers who do come aboard may save their best ideas for an outside consulting practice or spend their time looking for a better-paid job. Both problems are downstream of compensation design, and both are solvable. Teaching you to solve them is much of what this book is about.

There is a third job pay performs that the textbook tradition has often understated. Sinek (2009) argues that organizations attract people who care about the why of the work, not only the what. A compensation system designed only for incentive and sorting can recruit a workforce, but only a system that also visibly honors the mission tends to retain one. Chapter 7 returns to this tension when incentive design clashes with mission; Chapter 9 returns to it again under the heading of recognition and retention.

A second foundational principle is worth flagging at the outset. Labor is a derived demand. The Cambridge economist Alfred Marshall (1890) named the principle clearly more than a century ago: employers do not want labor for its own sake but for the value the labor produces. The wage one can command, then, is bounded above by the marginal contribution one's work makes to the output an employer (or, in the public sector, the public) values, and bounded below by the alternative wages available in the labor market. Chapter 5 returns to derived demand in the practical context of market pricing.

When Incentives Go Wrong

Compensation systems are powerful enough to cause real harm when they reward the wrong thing. The pharmaceutical company Novartis once paid its sales force almost entirely on volume: move more pills, earn more money. A federal investigation found that representatives were rewarded for prescriptions written regardless of whether they were medically appropriate, including prescriptions encouraged through sham speaker programs and kickbacks to high-prescribing physicians. The system produced exactly what it paid for, which was volume, generated unethically. In 2020 Novartis paid $678 million to settle, then overhauled its sales compensation to reward how sales were achieved, not merely that they were achieved (U.S. Department of Justice, 2020).

The same logic shows up in government. In 2014, staff at multiple Department of Veterans Affairs hospitals were found to be manipulating patient wait-time data. At its root this was a compensation-design failure: senior leaders' bonuses and ratings were tied to wait-time targets that staff learned to game (U.S. Department of Veterans Affairs, Office of Inspector General, 2014). Whenever pay is tied to a single number, ask the diagnostic question: what behavior is this actually rewarding, and what behavior is it implicitly punishing?

The conclusion is not to give up on incentives but to design them with eyes open. Brown (2012) frames the leadership stance the design demands: investing in people whose payoff is not guaranteed requires the courage to enter what she calls the arena. The alternative —

refusing to enter — guarantees the slower failure. The chapters that follow give the design discipline. Chapter 7 names the structural traps incentives produce, and Chapter 11 gives the measurement habits that catch them early.

> **FROM THE FIELD · DESIGNING PAY TO ATTRACT AND TO BEHAVE**
>
> Early in my career I worked in Silicon Valley at Sun Microsystems, where one of my projects was redesigning how we paid the sales force. To attract people from larger competitors such as IBM and Hewlett-Packard, we removed the commission caps those firms used. If you sold more million-dollar servers, your pay was not capped at what your boss made. It is also very hard to arrange kickbacks on million-dollar purchases, so the design rewarded real selling.
>
> Those servers helped power companies like E-Trade, Netflix, Amazon, and even Google. One Sun manager from those years, Eric Schmidt, went on to become Google's chief executive officer. We fine-tuned the plan almost every year, because each design change produced its own unintended consequences, a habit I would urge any manager to keep.

> **COMPENSATION MYTHS, AND WHAT IS ACTUALLY TRUE**
>
> **Myth:** People care only about money. **Reality:** Employees weigh fairness, flexibility, recognition, benefits, and growth alongside pay; once pay is competitive, those factors often decide who stays.
>
> **Myth:** Higher pay always improves performance. **Reality:** Poorly designed incentives can starve the work that is not measured and even invite gaming or misconduct; how a plan is designed matters more than how large it is.
>
> **Myth:** Compensation is an administrative cost to minimize. **Reality:** It is the largest controllable expense in most organizations and one of the strongest levers for performance and retention; treated as strategy, it earns its keep.

The DART Model

The organizing framework for this book is the **DART model**. DART stands for **Direction and Deployment of Talent**, **Assessment and Attraction of Talent**, **Rewarding and Retaining Talent**, and **Teaching and Transforming Talent**. The model proposes that organizational performance depends on how well talent is aligned to goals, how valuable that talent is when selected, how motivated employees are to contribute, and how effectively the organization develops people over time. A model matters because pay decisions are rarely isolated: base pay, incentives, benefits, recognition, promotion, and development all influence one another.

Organizational Performance (as a share of optimal) = D x A x R

This expression is intentionally simplified for teaching. D is Direction and Deployment, A is Assessment and Attraction, and R is Rewarding and Retaining. T, Teaching and Transforming, is a second-period activity that deepens the value of the talent attracted to join an organization (A). Hiring managers can assess and attract for current ability, future ability, or both. The multiplicative logic matters: if an employee spends only 50 percent of her time working on tasks and duties aligned with the organizational mission and works at 40 percent of her potential, the combined result is an employee working at 20 percent of her optimal potential. Suppose this employee could sell computer systems that generate $2 million in profit for the company at full potential. The employee we just described would generate $400,000 of profit. If the organization compensates her with a $40,000 bonus, a $100,000 salary, and benefits worth $60,000, it will likely continue to employ her, because the difference between the profit she generates and her compensation is still positive. Yet a reward system that never asks whether she could be better aligned to more productive behavior, or pushed to work harder, is impaired rather than merely average. In boom times there is no issue, but what if sudden changes put pressure on pricing and demand falls, cutting the profit on the same level of sales to $200,000? We now have a marginal case, with wages exactly equal to marginal productivity and no cushion for the organization to absorb risk. Such an organization may still function, but it does so as one of the 'walking wounded,' kept moving by improvisation and heroic effort even though the system itself is weak.

The multiplicative form is also why the manager matters so much. Buckingham and Coffman (1999) describe great managers as catalysts whose function is to speed up the reaction between an employee's talent and the organization's goals — accelerating several DART variables at once. Buckingham and Clifton (2001) extend the point: development concentrated in an employee's strengths produces compounding returns, while development spent fighting weaknesses tends to produce averages. Chapter 10 builds the practice; this chapter only flags where the leverage lives.

From the Field: A Note from the Harvard Class of 1992

Angela Duckworth and I were classmates in the Harvard Class of 1992. The argument she has developed in the years since — that perseverance and passion for very long-term goals predict outcomes that raw measured ability does not — sits behind the R in DART. The work of Rewarding and Retaining is not only to keep people from leaving; it is to make staying make sense for the people whose contribution depends on a long arc. Chapter 10 develops this idea around development and coaching; here in Chapter 1 it is enough to say that pay alone cannot manufacture grit, but the conditions compensation creates can either nourish it or starve it.

An example worth flagging here, and developing in Chapter 10. When I joined Procter & Gamble in 1992 — the same year Duckworth and I graduated — the company taught new hires that the future CEO had to come up the same brand-management ladder we were stepping onto. That architectural choice, that no senior role would be filled from outside, was what justified everything else in the iceberg-shaped compensation package, and it is the cleanest historical example of how compensation design and talent development can be built as one system rather than two.

Direction and Deployment

Direction and Deployment of Talent is the alignment between people and the work the organization needs done: job design, role clarity, performance expectations, and the placement of people on tasks and teams. It matters to compensation because rewards reinforce behavior. If success is not defined clearly, any incentive system will be blunt or easy to manipulate. A public agency may say it values service quality and collaboration, but if employees are rewarded mainly for individual output volume, the reward system will undercut the broader goal. Direction must come first; compensation should support it, not contradict it. A useful way to picture this is a sports roster: a good manager sets the lineup so each player stands where their strengths help the team most, moving an outfielder to second base or naming a designated hitter, while a player who coasts can drag down the effort of everyone around them. The same instinct underlies Jim Collins's advice to get the right people on the bus and in the right seats (Collins, 2001) and the strengths-based management popularized by Gallup's research, which holds that people contribute most when their roles fit their talents (Buckingham & Coffman, 1999; Buckingham & Clifton, 2001).

Assessment and Attraction

Assessment and Attraction of Talent concerns the value of the workforce the organization brings in and develops: identifying needs, evaluating jobs, judging current skill and future potential, and competing in the labor market. Compensation matters here because external competitiveness affects who applies and who accepts. Yet attraction is not only about paying more; it also involves pay structure, benefits, transparency, advancement opportunity, and the credibility of the employer's reward philosophy. This is also where Teaching and Transforming begins, because some employees are chosen for what they can do now and others for what they may be able to contribute in the future with experience, mentoring, and training.

Rewarding and Retaining

Rewarding and Retaining Talent is the center of this book. It concerns how organizations convert the value of talent into sustained performance through pay, incentives, benefits, recognition, and a fair employment experience. Because rewards are the most visible part of the system to employees, they strongly shape trust, motivation, and retention. The analytical toolkit we use throughout this part of DART is the pay model, introduced next.

Teaching and Transforming

Teaching and Transforming Talent is the organization's capacity to improve employee capability over time through onboarding, training, coaching, mentoring, stretch assignments, and leadership development. It is best understood as a second-period activity:

an organization first directs, assesses, attracts, deploys, and rewards the people it hopes to retain, then discovers whether it can increase the value of those employees by teaching them new skills and behaviors and helping them augment their abilities. One employer may hire the strongest immediate performer; another may hire a candidate with strong learning agility because the role is expected to change. The second employer is making an assessment decision that already assumes the future value of development. Because transformation is ultimately about durable habits rather than one-time training, it echoes the discipline Stephen Covey described in building highly effective habits (Covey, 1989).

Exhibit 1.1 · The DART Framework as a Workforce System

Exhibit 1.1 · The DART model as a connected workforce system, from strategy to performance and back.

The Pay Model: Objectives, Policy Choices, and Techniques

Within Rewarding and Retaining, the pay model gives us a structured way to design and judge any compensation system. It has three parts, and we will return to it throughout the book.

Objectives

First, the objectives, which are what the system is trying to achieve. Four are standard: efficiency, fairness, ethics, and compliance with the law. A well-designed system advances all four at once rather than trading one away for another.

Policy choices

Second, the policy choices, which are how the organization will get there. There are four. **Internal alignment** asks how jobs relate to one another inside the organization: should

Jose and Maria, doing the same job with the same experience, be paid the same? **External competitiveness** asks how pay compares with the outside market: if Jose and Maria learn that their friend Andrew earns fifty percent more elsewhere, they will spend their energy trying to find Andrew's job. **Employee contributions** ask how individual performance and skill drive pay. And **compensation management** asks how the whole system is administered and communicated.

Techniques

Third, the techniques, which are the specific tools that translate policy into paychecks: job evaluation, salary surveys, merit-pay plans, benefits design, and more. Later chapters explain each in turn, so do not worry if the terms are unfamiliar now.

The pay model is most useful as a place to ask the 'so what?' question. A former Sun chief executive, Scott McNealy, would meet recommendations with 'So what? Big deal. Who cares?' Whenever someone proposes a new pay practice, such as adding a signing bonus, switching to broadbanding, or capping executive pay, walk it through the model: does it serve our objectives, does it fit our policy choices, and is the technique well designed? If you cannot answer those three questions, the practice probably will not work.

The Forms of Pay

When people hear the word compensation, they picture base salary, the cash that lands in a checking account every two weeks. That is only part of the picture. **Total compensation** includes cash (base pay, merit increases, incentives, and cost-of-living adjustments), benefits (retirement, health care, paid leave, and family-friendly programs), and **relational returns**, the non-financial parts of the deal: recognition, status, employment security, challenging work, the chance to learn and grow, the people one works with, and the mission. In government and nonprofit work, relational returns often carry more weight than in the private sector, because mission is part of why people chose those careers in the first place.

> **FROM THE FIELD · CHOOSING RELATIONAL RETURNS**
>
> About nineteen years ago I turned down an offer from Google to join California State University, Dominguez Hills. The recruiter told me that, as far as she knew, no one had ever turned down a Google offer to work at a Cal State. The Google package, with its salary, bonus, stock, and famously good free food, was larger by every cash measure.
>
> I took the university position anyway, because the mission and the work were what I valued most. That is a relational return doing exactly what relational returns do, and it is a reminder not to let the biggest paycheck make a decision over the entire value of the compensation package.

Pay at the Bottom of the Market

Compensation is not only about engineers and executives. Most people work near the wage floor, and in California that floor is closely regulated. The car-wash industry is a telling example. The CLEAN Carwash Worker Center estimates that Los Angeles County alone has roughly five hundred car washes employing about ten thousand people, most earning at or near the state minimum wage, which reached $16.90 an hour in 2026 (CLEAN Carwash Worker Center, n.d.). California has long treated the industry as a high risk for wage theft, the unlawful denial of earned wages such as unpaid hours, overtime, or breaks. Under the state's Car Wash Worker Law, operators must register with the Labor Commissioner and post a surety bond, raised to $150,000, that funds back pay when workers are underpaid (California Department of Industrial Relations, n.d.). Designing pay at the bottom of the market means getting the legal floor right before anything else.

Behind that floor is a larger fact about the Southern California economy: it runs substantially on immigrant labor. Immigrants are roughly a third of California's workers (Public Policy Institute of California, 2025), and in the Los Angeles metropolitan area they hold close to two in five jobs, concentrated in industries such as construction, food service, caregiving, and car washing (USAFacts, 2024). That reality became vivid in 2025, when intensified federal immigration enforcement across Southern California, including sweeps at roughly two dozen car washes in Los Angeles and Orange Counties, pulled workers off the job and forced some businesses to close, whether because employees were detained or because they stayed home in fear (Associated Press, 2025). For a compensation manager, the lesson is that pay operates inside a labor market shaped by law, migration, and enforcement, not by wage rates alone. The people who staff California's car washes, kitchens, farms, and construction sites are central to how the state's economy runs, and how they are paid is a compensation question, not a footnote.

Stakeholder Perspectives

Compensation looks different depending on who is looking. Society cares about productivity and fairness in the tax burden. Owners and stockholders care about whether pay, especially executive pay, aligns with performance. Customers, in most cases, want low prices, which depend in part on labor costs; remember that labor is a derived demand, and an organization exists to serve a purpose, a university to educate students or a retailer to serve customers, not simply to pay its people. Managers see compensation as both a major expense to control and a tool to influence behavior. Employees see it as a return for their work and a measure of how the organization values them. These perspectives are not always compatible, and a good compensation system has to navigate the trade-offs among them.

Why This Text Centers Rewards

DART includes all four elements because performance depends on the whole system, but a compensation textbook should focus on the part of the system that compensation influences most directly. Rewarding and Retaining is therefore the center of this book, while Direction and Deployment, Assessment and Attraction, and Teaching and Transforming provide the strategic context. This focus reflects the practical needs of managers and HR professionals, whose hardest decisions involve pay philosophy, salary structures, market pricing, incentive design, benefits trade-offs, pay compression, equity concerns, and the development that supports retention. These are reward decisions, but they cannot be handled well unless the reader sees how they connect to organizational goals, talent value, and workforce growth.

> **CALIFORNIA SPOTLIGHT · REWARD DESIGN UNDER TRANSPARENCY AND EQUAL PAY**
>
> California is an especially important setting for compensation because legal requirements increasingly shape reward design, and they do more than create compliance tasks; they push organizations toward clearer pay philosophies and more disciplined structures.
>
> **Pay scale disclosure.** Under Senate Bill 1162 (effective 2023), employers with fifteen or more employees generally must include the pay scale in job postings, and any employee may request the pay scale for their current position.
>
> **Pay data reporting.** Employers with 100 or more employees must file an annual pay data report with the California Civil Rights Department, due in mid-May each year, which creates pressure to review pay structures systematically (California Civil Rights Department, 2025). A new law expands the report from ten job categories to twenty-three beginning with the 2027 reporting year, requiring finer pay and demographic detail.
>
> **Equal pay.** The California Equal Pay Act prohibits unlawful pay differences for substantially similar work and limits the defenses an employer may raise (California Department of Industrial Relations, 2025).
>
> **A link to development.** California also supports employer-driven training through the Employment Training Panel, reinforcing that reward and development belong together (California Employment Training Panel, n.d.).

What Follows in This Book

The remaining chapters build from DART and the pay model into the specific tools of compensation practice. Early chapters explain the theory of compensation, the California environment, and the logic of compensation strategy. Later chapters address job valuation, salary structures, market pricing, base-pay administration, incentives, benefits, development-linked retention, and reward metrics. Throughout, the guiding question stays the same: how can organizations reward talent in ways that improve performance while remaining fair, competitive, and legally sound? The answer is rarely a single pay tactic. More often it is a coherent reward system that fits strategy, labor markets, employee expectations, organizational values, and the organization's capacity to develop talent over time.

A note on the coaching thread that runs through the book. Several chapters draw on a connected set of sources from the coaching, positive-psychology, hospitality, and continuous-performance-management literatures. Chapter 7 (Incentive Pay and Performance Management) develops Doerr's (2018) Objectives and Key Results, paired with his CFRs — Conversations, Feedback, Recognition — as the modern alternative to the annual review. Chapter 9 (Recognition, Retention, and Employee Experience) builds on Froh and Bono's (2014) research on gratitude as a developable manager skill, alongside Guidara's (2022) one-size-fits-one principle from the hospitality industry. Chapter 10 (Teaching and Transforming Talent) anchors strengths-based development in Buckingham and Clifton (2001) and Buckingham and Coffman (1999), and pairs that work with Brown (2012) on the vulnerability the manager-as-coach role requires. Chapter 11 (Measuring Reward System Effectiveness) closes the loop with Doerr's measurement discipline and Sinek's (2019) finite-versus-infinite-game distinction. The DART model is the organizing skeleton; these sources are the muscles that move it.

Key Terms

The following terms, set in bold throughout the chapter, anchor the framework.

Term	Definition
Compensation	The pay employees receive directly and indirectly through wages, salaries, incentives, and benefits.
Total compensation	Cash (base, merit, incentives, cost-of-living) plus benefits plus relational returns.
Relational returns	The non-financial value of work: recognition, status, security, challenge, growth, colleagues, and mission.
DART model	Thomas J. Norman's organizing framework: Direction and Deployment, Assessment and Attraction, Rewarding and Retaining, and Teaching and Transforming of talent.
Incentive function	Compensation's effect on what employees do once on the payroll.
Sorting function	Compensation's effect on who applies, accepts, and stays.
Derived demand	The principle that labor is demanded only because of the value its output creates for employers or the public.
Pay model	The toolkit of objectives, policy choices, and techniques used to design and judge a compensation system.
Compensation objectives	Efficiency, fairness, ethics, and compliance.
Policy choices	Internal alignment, external competitiveness, employee contributions, and management.
Internal alignment	The consistency of pay relationships across jobs inside the organization.
External competitiveness	How an organization's pay compares with relevant labor markets.
Pay transparency	The practice or legal requirement of disclosing compensation information, such as pay ranges.
Wage theft	The unlawful denial of earned wages, such as unpaid hours, overtime, or breaks.
Retention	The ability to keep employees, especially those whose departure would reduce performance or raise replacement costs.

Discussion Questions

1. How does compensation function as both an incentive and a sorting mechanism, and why does that distinction matter for public managers?
2. Choose two stakeholder perspectives and explain where their definitions of good compensation conflict and where they agree. Ground your answer in a public-sector example if you can.
3. Why does the DART model treat organizational performance as a multiplicative system rather than a set of independent activities?
4. Walk a real organization (ideally one where you have worked) through the pay model: its objectives, policy choices, and techniques.
5. Why might a market-competitive pay system still fail to retain or develop talent?
6. In what ways do California pay transparency rules change how an employer should think about salary structures?
7. Hyundai and Kia built rapid United States growth on a low-cost manufacturing model. Using the idea of derived demand and the two functions of pay, explain what the strategy gained and what it ultimately cost.
8. California's car-wash enforcement and its immigrant-heavy low-wage workforce show that most workers earn near the wage floor. What legal and ethical responsibilities does that create for a compensation manager?

Applied Exercise

A medium-sized California employer says its strategy depends on innovation, collaboration, and retaining high-skill employees. Its managers, however, make pay decisions case by case, job postings rarely show clear ranges, the organization provides little structured development, and employees complain that raises seem inconsistent. Using the DART model, identify each of the following:

1. One problem related to Direction and Deployment of Talent.
2. One problem related to Assessment and Attraction of Talent.
3. Two problems related to Rewarding and Retaining Talent.
4. One problem related to Teaching and Transforming Talent.
5. Two compensation actions and one developmental action that would improve alignment between the employer's goals and its talent system.

References

ABC7 Los Angeles. (2023). *LAUSD, teachers union reach tentative labor agreement that includes salary increase, smaller class sizes.* https://abc7.com/lausd-teachers-union-labor-agreement-utla/13149284/

Associated Press. (2025, June 20). *More LA car washes targeted in immigration raids, some closed amid fears of further sweeps.* The Spokesman-Review. https://www.spokesman.com/stories/2025/jun/20/more-la-car-washes-targeted-in-immigration-raids-s/

Brown, B. (2012). Daring greatly: How the courage to be vulnerable transforms the way we live, love, parent, and lead. Gotham Books.

Buckingham, M., & Clifton, D. O. (2001). *Now, discover your strengths.* Free Press.

Buckingham, M., & Coffman, C. (1999). *First, break all the rules: What the world's greatest managers do differently.* Simon & Schuster.

California Civil Rights Department. (2025). *Pay data reporting.* https://calcivilrights.ca.gov/paydatareporting/

California Department of Industrial Relations. (n.d.). *Rules and regulations: For car washing and polishing.* https://www.dir.ca.gov/DLSE/Car_Wash_Rules_Regs.html

California Department of Industrial Relations. (2025). *California Equal Pay Act.* https://www.dir.ca.gov/dlse/california_equal_pay_act.htm

California Employment Training Panel. (n.d.). *About ETP.* https://etp.ca.gov/

CLEAN Carwash Worker Center. (n.d.). *About.* https://www.cleancarwash.org/

Clifton, J., & Harter, J. (2019). It's the manager: Gallup finds the quality of managers and team leaders is the single biggest factor in your organization's long-term success. Gallup Press.

CNN. (2025, September 8). *Nearly 500 workers were taken in a raid at Hyundai's battery plant. In a quiet Georgia town, the silence is deafening.* https://www.cnn.com/2025/09/08/us/georgia-hyundai-ice-raid-community

Collins, J. (2001). *Good to great: Why some companies make the leap... and others don't.* HarperBusiness.

Covey, S. R. (1989). *The 7 habits of highly effective people.* Free Press.

Doerr, J. (2018). Measure what matters: How Google, Bono, and the Gates Foundation rock the world with OKRs. Portfolio.

Duckworth, A. (2016). Grit: The power of passion and perseverance. Scribner.

Froh, J. J., & Bono, G. (2014). Making grateful kids: The science of building character. Templeton Press.

Guidara, W. (2022). Unreasonable hospitality: The remarkable power of giving people more than they expect. Optimism Press.

LAist. (2023). *Big changes to come for LAUSD teachers and support staff as two labor deals move forward.* https://laist.com/news/education/united-teachers-los-angeles-teachers-contract-deal-los-angeles-unified-school-district-2023

Marshall, A. (1890). Principles of economics. Macmillan.

Public Policy Institute of California. (2025). *Immigrants and the labor market.* https://www.ppic.org/publication/immigrants-and-the-labor-market/

Sinek, S. (2009). Start with why: How great leaders inspire everyone to take action. Portfolio.

Sinek, S. (2019). The infinite game. Portfolio.

Society for Human Resource Management. (n.d.). *Total rewards.* https://www.shrm.org/

U.S. Department of Justice. (2020, July 1). *Novartis pays $678 million to settle False Claims Act allegations of illegal kickbacks involving sham speaker programs.* https://www.justice.gov/usao-sdny

U.S. Department of Labor. (2024, May 30). *US Department of Labor files complaint to stop Hyundai manufacturer, partners from using, profiting from oppressive child labor* [News release]. https://www.dol.gov/newsroom/releases/whd/whd20240530

U.S. Department of Veterans Affairs, Office of Inspector General. (2014). *Review of alleged patient deaths, patient wait times, and scheduling practices at the Phoenix VA Health Care System.* https://www.vaoig.gov/reports/audit/review-alleged-patient-deaths-patient-wait-times-and-scheduling-practices-phoenix-va

USAFacts. (2024). *What percent of jobs in the Los Angeles, CA area are held by immigrants?* https://usafacts.org/answers/what-percent-of-jobs-in-the-us-are-held-by-immigrants/metro-area/los-angeles-ca/

COMPENSATION: REWARDING AND RETAINING TALENT · CALIFORNIA EDITION
CHAPTER 2

Chapter 2. Compensation Strategy, Theory, and Philosophy

Best fit, not just best practices.

Thomas J. Norman, Ph.D.

Photograph by Thomas J. Norman

OPENING CASE · THREE COMPANIES, THREE STRATEGIES

Three successful organizations, three completely different ways of paying people. Google sits at the top of the technology labor market with strong base salaries, generous equity, and famous perks, because its advantage is software written by elite engineers and the business cannot run on average talent. Nucor Steel pays a relatively modest base but adds a productivity bonus that can nearly double take-home pay in a good year, because Nucor competes on cost per ton and wants every worker invested in output and quality.

Merrill Lynch, in the years before the 2008 financial crisis, paid its brokers almost entirely on commission, rewarding the 'hunters' who brought in client assets. None of the three copied the others, and all three were right, because each firm's compensation strategy followed its business strategy.

That is the central lesson of this chapter: there is no universally best way to pay. There is only the way that fits.

Learning Objectives

After studying this chapter, you should be able to do the following:

1. Describe the main theories underlying compensation and connect them to the DART model.
2. Explain the four policy choices and the lead, lag, and match market postures.
3. Apply the four-step strategy process, the AMO equation, and the three tests to a real organization.
4. Analyze how pay-for-performance and equity strategies play out at the top of the market, and the governance questions they raise.
5. Evaluate why no single compensation approach works in every organization.

What Strategy Means

A strategy is a coherent set of decisions about how an organization will compete and win. It states what the organization will do, what it will not do, and how it will be different from its peers. A compensation strategy is the part of that picture concerned with pay: how the organization will use rewards to attract, motivate, and keep the people the larger strategy requires. The cardinal rule is fit. Compensation strategy follows business strategy, never the other way around, which is why the same pay plan can be brilliant at one organization and ruinous at another.

Two contemporary framings help students hold strategy in the right shape. Doerr (2018) reminds the strategist that "ideas are easy; execution is everything," a corrective for the textbook tendency to treat strategy as the writing of intent rather than the wiring of action. Sinek (2019) supplies the time-horizon corrective. A strategy designed for an infinite game — public missions, education, public health, and any organization expected to endure beyond its current leadership — must be measured differently than one designed for a finite contest with a terminal scoreboard. Compensation strategy inherits both warnings: it must be executable, and it must be honest about whether the game it is funding has an end.

The Theories Behind the Strategy

Why would the design of pay change what people do? Several theories, introduced here and revisited later, each explain part of the answer, and real strategies usually draw on more than one.

Agency theory. In the 1987 film Wall Street, the financier Gordon Gekko tells a room of shareholders that greed, the pursuit of self-interest, 'clarifies' and drives progress. Beneath the bravado is a real idea. Agency theory holds that owners (principals) must design pay so that the self-interest of executives and employees (agents) aligns with the owners' interests (Jensen & Meckling, 1976). Much of incentive design is an answer to this agency problem, and we return to it in the chapter on pay for performance.

Equity theory holds that people compare their own ratio of contribution to reward against the ratios they see in others, and act to restore balance when it feels unfair (Adams, 1965). **Tournament theory** holds that large differentials act like prizes that intensify competition to advance (Lazear & Rosen, 1981). **Expectancy theory** holds that people put out effort only when they believe effort will produce performance, performance will produce a reward, and the reward is something they value (Vroom, 1964).

From the Field: The Copy Machine, Early in My Career

Equity theory is easy to teach and harder to live with. I learned it at a copy machine. Early in my career, before pay transparency was a norm and before California had any of the disclosure rules it has now, someone left an offer letter on the glass. The new hire — a woman who had started two weeks before me, in a role broadly similar to mine — had been hired at two thousand dollars more than I was earning. The information was a few seconds of accident, but the feeling it produced was immediate and durable. It changed nothing about the work I did, the value I created, or the relationship between me and my employer, but it changed how I thought about all three.

The lesson for students is straightforward, and it is the only piece of compensation advice I give the same way every year: always negotiate, and ask for what you want. When the hiring manager asked me what I wanted to be paid, I knew the published range, but I was excited about the offer and trusted the manager to give me something fair. He did, in a way — but not as fair as the offer he gave a candidate who asked. The asymmetry was structural. The manager's budget was finite. The candidate who asked got more of it; the candidate who deferred got the residual.

The story is more interesting than the standard gendered narrative around negotiation because, in my case, the woman got more. The popular reading from Babcock and Laschever (2003) is that women on average ask less and lose out — and that pattern is real and well-documented. Here, though, one woman asked and one man trusted, and the result was the predictable inverse. The lesson is not about gender; it is about the negotiating posture. As an employee, treat the offer conversation as a one-shot game and prepare for it as such; you will not get the same chance again for years. As a designer of compensation systems, recognize that opaque offer practices systematically transfer wealth toward candidates who ask, in whichever direction the asking happens to run. Chapter 3 returns to the California pay-transparency rules that now exist precisely because this asymmetry produced predictable patterns of inequity, and Chapter 5 returns to the market-pricing and negotiation discipline the candidate side should use.

Human capital theory holds that pay reflects the value of the skills and knowledge a person brings and the investment required to build them (Becker, 1964). And **institutional theory** holds that organizations often adopt pay practices simply because those practices are normal in their field (DiMaggio & Powell, 1983). Each theory is a lens; in the language of the DART model, together they explain how Rewarding and Retaining actually moves behavior.

The Four Policy Choices

Every compensation strategy answers the same four questions introduced with the pay model in Chapter 1. **Internal alignment** sets how jobs relate to one another inside the organization. **External competitiveness** sets how pay compares with the outside market. **Employee contributions** sets how individual performance and skill drive pay. And **management** sets how the system is administered and communicated. A compensation strategy is, in large part, a consistent set of answers to these four.

Best Fit, Not Just Best Practices

There are two broad philosophies for designing a compensation strategy. **Best practices** means copying what successful organizations do, on the theory that the market has already validated those choices. **Best fit** means designing for your own context: your strategy, workforce, competitive environment, and mission.

Both have a place, but they apply to different parts of the system. Best practices travel well for the technical infrastructure of compensation, the parts that simply must be done correctly: meeting legal requirements, using sound salary-survey methodology, administering benefits competently. You will not gain an advantage by doing those better than everyone else; you avoid disaster by doing them at all. Best fit is where you actually compete: incentive design, the mix of cash and benefits, and the relational returns discussed in Chapter 1. Copying Google's compensation strategy at a municipal Department of Water and Power would be a categorical error, because the mission, funding, workforce, and talent market are entirely different.

Lafley and Martin (2013) give the five-question version of this discipline. Strategy, in their formulation, requires answering five interrelated choices: What is our winning aspiration? Where will we play? How will we win? What capabilities must we have in place? And what management systems are required? Compensation is rarely the first of those five questions, but it is almost always the fifth — the management system through which capability, position, and aspiration are funded, signaled, and sustained. A reward design that cannot articulate its place in those five answers is not yet a strategy; it is an inheritance.

A Strategy Matrix: One Logic, Many Systems

Because compensation must fit strategy, organizations pursuing different strategies build very different pay systems, and none is universally best. A company competing on innovation reaches for aggressive market pay, equity, and scarce-skill premiums; one competing on cost emphasizes standardized structures and tight labor-cost control. The matrix in Exhibit 2.1 maps the most common patterns. The point is not to memorize cells but to see the logic: each pay system is an answer to one question, namely what behavior does our strategy require, and how does pay make that behavior more likely?

Exhibit 2.1 · Compensation Strategy Matrix

Organizational Strategy	Compensation Characteristics	Example Organizations
Cost Leadership	Tight pay control, standardized jobs, efficiency focus	Walmart; Amazon fulfillment
Innovation	High incentives, equity pay, scarce-skill premiums	Google; Nvidia; 3M
Customer Service	Higher wages, retention focus, investment in development	Costco; Southwest Airlines
Public Service	Stability, pensions, structured step progression	Government agencies; public schools
High-Risk Growth	Equity-heavy pay, aggressive incentives, upside over base	Startups; venture-backed firms

Exhibit 2.1 · How organizational strategy shapes compensation characteristics.

Consider 3M, the Minnesota manufacturer behind Scotch Tape and the Post-it Note. Its strategy is relentless innovation, and its reward system is built to produce it. For decades 3M has encouraged technical employees to spend up to 15 percent of their time on projects of their own choosing, the famous '15 percent time' that gave rise to the Post-it Note. That autonomy is itself a reward, a noncash form of pay that signals what the company values. The company reinforces the message through recognition as much as cash: election to the Carlton Society, its internal 'Nobel Prize' for scientists, is among its highest honors. And it holds the whole system accountable to a single public number, the long-standing goal that a substantial share of revenue, historically about 30 percent, come from products launched within the previous four years. The lesson for compensation strategy is that an innovation firm pays for invention with a deliberate blend of cash, autonomy, and recognition, tying line of sight not to hours worked but to new ideas that reach the market.

> **MINI CASE · WHEN INCENTIVES UNDERMINED COLLABORATION**
> A technology company rewarded individual sales almost entirely through large commissions and a forced ranking. Short-term sales jumped. But salespeople stopped sharing leads and information, departments competed instead of cooperating, customer complaints climbed, and turnover rose. The plan worked exactly as designed: it maximized individual output. The trouble was that the strategy needed collaboration and durable customer relationships, and the pay system rewarded neither. The failure was not the incentive's strength; it was its misalignment with the strategy the company actually pursued.

Paying for Skills, Not Just Titles

A job title is a convenient label, but it is a crude guide to value. Two people with the same title can hold very different skills, and the skills an organization most needs are often the ones changing fastest. A growing strategic choice, especially for roles built on scarce or emerging capabilities, is to price the skill rather than the title: to ask what the market pays for a specific, in-demand capability and to reward the people who hold it accordingly. This is the logic behind the premium that data, cybersecurity, and artificial-intelligence skills command, and it is why the Databricks case later in this chapter is a talent strategy as much as a pay decision.

Pricing skills well requires moving faster than the annual salary survey. Markets for hot skills can shift within a single hiring cycle, so organizations increasingly blend traditional survey data with real-time market signals, such as live job-posting pay ranges and offer-acceptance rates, to stay current. Speed, though, needs discipline. Premium pay for a scarce skill should be governed by clear guardrails: a written rationale for when a premium is warranted, an approval process so that exceptions do not quietly become the rule, and a plan to fold the premium back into the structure if the skill becomes common. Without those guardrails, today's retention fix becomes tomorrow's internal-equity problem.

The opposite error is overreacting to noise. A skill that spikes in one quarter may cool the next, and chasing every fluctuation can destabilize a structure and erode the trust that internal alignment depends on. The strategic posture is to distinguish a durable shift in the value of a skill, which deserves a structural response, from short-term volatility, which usually does not. In DART terms, paying for skills is an Assessment-and-Attraction decision with direct consequences for Rewarding and Retaining: it determines whether the organization can attract scarce talent without paying everyone else unfairly.

Skills-Based Pay and the Future of Work

Traditional pay systems reward job title, hierarchy, and tenure. A growing number of organizations instead pay for skills, competencies, certifications, and capabilities, from cloud and cybersecurity credentials to project-management certificates, bilingual ability, and AI-related technical skills. The logic is that in fast-changing fields, skills become obsolete faster than job titles do, so paying for current, scarce capability keeps a workforce adaptable in a way that paying for position cannot. Exhibit 2.2 contrasts the two approaches. Skills-based pay is not a wholesale replacement for job-based pay, but as work changes faster than the org chart, the share of pay tied to demonstrated capability is rising.

Exhibit 2.2 · Job-Based Pay vs. Skills-Based Pay

Traditional Job-Based Pay	Skills-Based Pay
Pay tied to job title and grade	Pay tied to demonstrated skills and competencies
Large raises require a promotion	Acquiring a valued skill raises pay
Hierarchical, ladder progression	Flexible, lattice development pathways
Stable, slowly changing job definitions	Rapidly evolving, certifiable skill needs

Exhibit 2.2 · Job-based pay rewards position; skills-based pay rewards capability.

The Four-Step Strategy Process

Organizations move from 'we should have a compensation strategy' to a real one through four steps. **Assess:** where are we now, what does our current pay say about what we value, where are we losing candidates and employees, and what does the relevant labor market actually pay? **Choose:** given that assessment, where will we lead, where will we match, where are we willing to lag, and what message must our pay send? **Implement:** translate those choices into specific salary levels, ranges, and policies. This is where most strategies fail, not because the strategy was wrong, but because the hand-off to the managers who administer it broke down. **Reassess:** labor markets, missions, and competitive contexts change, so a strategy that fit five years ago may be wrong today. Public agencies should reassess at least every five years; a common and fair criticism is that they change far too rarely.

> **FROM THE FIELD · WHERE THE STRATEGY LIVES, THE PAY FOLLOWS**
>
> When I moved into human resources in Silicon Valley, I was a little disappointed to learn that we did not lead the market in HR pay. The company led in engineering and computer science, because that is where its competitive advantage lived. HR was above market with good bonuses, but one level below the engineers and programmers because we were support, not the core of the business. Once I understood the strategy, the pay

> made perfect sense. That realization is the Assess step doing its job: pay reflects where an organization competes to win.

Why Pay Alone Is Never Enough: AMO

One equation explains why a generous pay plan sometimes changes nothing. Performance is a product of ability, motivation, and opportunity: **A x M x O** (Appelbaum et al., 2000). The key word is product. If any one term is zero, the result is zero. The most generous bonus in the world will not give an average player the ability to score in the NBA, because the ability is missing; no incentive can manufacture a skill a person does not have. Broken processes, missing tools, or a manager who blocks good ideas destroy opportunity, and pay cannot unlock it either. Opportunity also includes the softer conditions for good work: a climate where people feel safe to raise problems and propose ideas, paired with enough structure that the freedom is usable; where that climate is missing, no bonus will substitute for it. Pay can move motivation, and only motivation. So diagnose in order: does the person have the ability? Do they have the opportunity? Only then is compensation a serious lever.

Vicious and Virtuous Circles

Compensation strategy is easiest to see when a cycle takes hold. A vicious circle feeds on itself. In a large school district, vacancies overload the staff who remain, the overload drives more departures, and each exit makes the next vacancy harder to fill, while enrollment-based funding and a high cost of living tighten the very budget that might fix it. Single fixes rarely break a cycle like that.

Then and Now: The LAUSD Reform Arc

The Los Angeles Unified School District case complicates the vicious-circle story this chapter started with. The compensation response was substantial. In 2023, LAUSD reached a three-year agreement with United Teachers Los Angeles providing a 21 percent salary increase over the contract period, smaller class sizes, and targeted increases for nurses, psychologists, counselors, special-education teachers, and early-education teachers. By July 2025, the average teacher salary reached approximately $106,000 (ABC7 Los Angeles, 2023; California Globe, 2023). A separate three-day strike by SEIU Local 99 — bus drivers, cafeteria workers, classroom assistants, and other support staff — produced an additional 30 percent wage increase, a district minimum wage of $22.52 per hour above both the City of Los Angeles and California minimums, and health-benefit access for part-time employees working four or more hours per day (LAist, 2023). For a moment, the cycle looked like it might break.

What complicated the picture was demographic and fiscal. Since the start of the COVID-19 pandemic in 2020, LAUSD enrollment has dropped by roughly 75,000 students, or 18 percent, falling to about 408,000 by 2025–2026 from a 2002 peak of 746,831. The federal pandemic-relief funds that helped support the new contracts have largely expired. In 2026, the LAUSD board voted to approve a reduction-in-force plan that could send layoff notices to as many as 3,200 employees, with about 650 layoffs expected (EdSource, 2026). At the same time, voluntary separations from LAUSD nearly doubled between 2021–2022 and 2023, the median tenure of educators who separated declined to roughly four years, and approximately 1,151 vacancies remained unfilled at the close of the school year.

The teaching point this case adds to the comparative set is harder than the simple reform-success or reform-failure binary. The 2023 compensation interventions did what compensation interventions can do: they raised the floor under pay enough that the recruitment-and-retention crisis stopped accelerating. What they could not do is reverse the underlying structural problem — declining enrollment combined with the loss of pandemic-era funding — which has produced the unusual combination of significant unfilled vacancies and a district-wide reduction in force in the same year. For students designing public-sector compensation strategies, the lesson is that pay reforms have to be situated in the demographic and fiscal context of the institution receiving them. A pay increase pursued without a credible plan for how it will be funded as one-time money expires can solve the immediate retention problem while creating a second-order layoff problem two years out. The vicious circle was not so much broken as transferred.

A virtuous circle runs the other way. Facing a serious shortage of air traffic controllers, the Federal Aviation Administration did not reach for one lever. Its 2025-2028 workforce plan combined a roughly thirty percent increase in Academy starting pay, completion and hard-to-staff awards of $5,000 to $10,000, a retention bonus worth twenty percent of pay for controllers who delayed retirement, and a streamlined hiring process that cut months from the timeline (Federal Aviation Administration, 2025). The contrast is the lesson: a multi-lever strategy that fits the problem can break a cycle that piecemeal fixes cannot.

Then and Now: The FAA Virtuous-Circle Outcome

The FAA case offers the comparative set's clearest example of a virtuous circle reinforced by sustained, multi-lever investment. The 2025–2028 Workforce Plan committed to hiring approximately 8,900 controllers over the period, including 2,000 in fiscal year 2025, 2,200 in FY 2026, 2,300 in FY 2027, and 2,400 in FY 2028 (Federal Aviation Administration, 2025). The agency executed against the plan and exceeded its first-year target: 2,028 controller trainees were hired in FY 2025, the highest annual total since 2008 (U.S. Department of Transportation, 2025).

What made the plan distinctive was that compensation was one of several reinforcing tools rather than the only one. The FAA raised Academy starting salaries by approximately 30 percent and added retention bonuses that kept nearly 400 retirement-eligible controllers in their seats. At the same time, the agency expanded Academy capacity (600 trainees in August 2025 alone, a record), streamlined its hiring process from eight steps to five (cutting time-to-hire by more than five months), and added financial incentives tied to placement at hard-to-staff facilities (Federal Aviation Administration, 2025). The deployed workforce reached approximately 11,000 Certified Professional Controllers by April 2026, with another 4,000 in the training pipeline, against a forecast staffing target of 12,563.

The picture is not unqualified success. A 2026 Government Accountability Office review found that the FAA still needed to establish clearer hiring goals and assess its hiring processes more rigorously (U.S. Government Accountability Office, 2026). The agency remains roughly twelve percent short of its full staffing target, and chronic overtime continues to drive fatigue and burnout that the new pipeline has not yet fully relieved. Even so, the FAA case is the cleanest counterexample in this chapter to the LAUSD outcome: a public agency facing a serious shortage of skilled labor moved on compensation, training capacity, process design, and retention at the same time, and the curve has begun to bend.

The pair of then-and-now sidebars now reads as a single teaching unit. LAUSD raised pay generously and saw the recruitment-and-retention crisis stabilize, only to find that pay reform could not reverse the larger demographic and fiscal pressures that produced the original cycle. The FAA paired compensation reform with capacity, process, and retention investment, and the staffing curve responded. For students designing public-sector compensation strategy, the takeaway is that pay matters and is necessary, but is rarely sufficient. A pay increase that arrives without complementary investment in training, process, and the conditions of work tends to look promising in the short term and disappointing later. A pay increase that arrives alongside those investments tends to compound them.

Three Tests for a Compensation Strategy

Whenever someone proposes a compensation strategy or a change to one, put it through three tests. The **alignment test** asks whether the strategy fits the mission and the rest of the organization's strategy; misaligned compensation produces misaligned behavior. The **differentiation test** asks whether the approach actually distinguishes the organization where distinction matters; paying the market median for everything is a default, not a strategy. A custodial role with straightforward work may call for simple market pay, while a parks manager who can grow outside revenue through rentals and youth programs is worth an incentive that rewards that growth. The **value test** asks whether the effort produces a measurable result, such as lower turnover, higher productivity, or fewer compliance failures, that justifies the cost. In one real case, a city had cut its workers' compensation specialists so deeply that it missed legal deadlines and paid fines far larger than the salaries it had saved; the value test would have caught that long before.

The tests apply not only to a new strategy but to the question of when an old one needs to evolve. Procter & Gamble, the archetypal 1980s–1990s lifetime-career employer, illustrates both halves. The classic system answered the alignment, differentiation, and value tests beautifully for its era — long careers, deep developmental investment, a stock-heavy deferred package that made staying obvious — but the same answers needed updating after the late-1990s leadership crisis. Under A.G. Lafley the company moved toward Connect + Develop open innovation, more external hiring for digital and analytic capabilities, and a more market-benchmarked compensation philosophy appropriate to shorter contemporary careers (Lafley & Charan, 2008; Lafley & Martin, 2013). The architectural insight survived; the implementation did not. Chapter 8 develops the iceberg framing, and Chapter 10 develops the promote-from-within architecture, with the same then-and-now caveat.

Compensation Philosophy

Before an organization builds structures, surveys, or incentive plans, it should be able to state a compensation philosophy: a short, formal statement of how it intends to pay, what it values, and how pay supports strategy. A clear philosophy turns scattered decisions into a coherent system and gives managers a reference when hard cases arise. A useful philosophy answers a handful of questions explicitly. Will the organization lead, match, or lag the market, and for which roles? How much of pay should depend on performance, and on whose performance, the individual's or the team's? How much weight goes to internal equity versus external competitiveness? How transparent will pay be? Organizations that can answer these questions in writing build pay systems that are consistent and defensible; those that cannot tend to drift, deciding each case on its own and accumulating the contradictions that later read as unfairness.

Pay Philosophy: Lead, Lag, and Match

A compensation philosophy states in advance where the organization wants to sit relative to the market. To **lead** is to pay above market, which fits roles that are scarce, critical, or central to competitive advantage. To **lag** is to pay below market, sometimes a deliberate choice when cost control is paramount or other rewards compensate. To **match** is to pay at market, the right call for most roles most of the time. Few organizations choose one posture for everyone; the art is deciding which roles to lead, which to match, and which can lag. In the public sector, where cash often cannot lead, managers lean on other levers: defined-benefit pensions through systems such as CalPERS and CalSTRS, job security, the pull of mission, and flexibilities such as telework, where California's public agencies have often moved ahead of private employers.

Strategy at the Extreme: Paying for Performance and Paying in Equity

The same strategic logic that sets a clerk's pay also governs the largest packages in the world. At the top of the market two philosophies dominate, paying for performance and paying in equity, and both show fit, and its limits, in sharp relief.

Pay for performance, taken to the limit

Tesla's 2018 award for chief executive Elon Musk, valued near $55.8 billion, paid him nothing unless the company hit a ladder of demanding market-capitalization and operational milestones; he earned the tranches as Tesla's value multiplied. The design is agency theory and the lead posture carried to their outer edge: tie nearly all of a leader's reward to shareholder outcomes. Yet the case also exposes the limits. A Delaware court voided the award in 2024 over the board's independence and the process used to set it, before the Delaware Supreme Court reinstated it in 2025 (Electrek, 2025). In November 2025, shareholders approved a new package worth up to roughly $1 trillion over ten years, tied to an $8.5 trillion market-capitalization target and operational milestones, with more than seventy-five percent in favor (CNBC, 2025a). Run it through the three tests: alignment is strong, but the differentiation and value tests raise hard questions about who sets the target, whether the board is truly independent, and whether the result justifies the cost.

Equity as the strategy

For many of the most sought-after employers, the strategy is equity itself. Databricks, still privately held and valued near $134 billion at the end of 2025, pays heavily in restricted stock units that do not turn into cash until a liquidity event, and it runs periodic employee tender offers so staff can sell shares before any public offering, an engineered-liquidity strategy aimed squarely at attracting and keeping scarce artificial-intelligence talent (CNBC, 2025b). The public-market mirror image is Oracle's co-founder Larry Ellison, whose roughly forty percent ownership stake briefly made him the world's richest person in September 2025 when Oracle's stock surged on AI demand, then shed tens of billions days later as doubts set in (Fortune, 2025). Both illustrate the same bet, that ownership aligns people with long-run value, and the same risk, that equity's worth swings with the market and can demotivate as quickly as it motivates. In DART terms, equity is a Rewarding-and-Retaining tool whose power depends entirely on fit with the firm's stage, volatility, and workforce.

> **CALIFORNIA SPOTLIGHT · A NEW COMPETITOR FOR POLICE RECRUITS**
>
> Compensation strategy plays out in real labor markets, and those markets can shift quickly. The Los Angeles Police Department spent years competing for a shrinking pool of recruits; its sworn ranks fell by more than a thousand in three years, and a 2023 contract raised a recruit's starting pay by about thirteen percent, to roughly $86,000, to compete (ABC7 Los Angeles, 2023).
>
> In 2025 a new and well-funded competitor entered the same labor market. As part of a large federal expansion, U.S. Immigration and Customs Enforcement launched an aggressive hiring campaign offering signing bonuses of up to $50,000, backed by a budget increase many times its prior level; reporting noted the campaign could pull officers and recruits away from local police departments (FactCheck.org, 2026; NBC News, 2025).
>
> The point here is not about immigration policy. It is that a federal agency dangling $50,000 bonuses is exactly the external-competitiveness shock the Assess step exists to

catch. It changes who applies, who stays, and what a city must offer to compete, and a strategy set in isolation can be overtaken almost overnight.

Public-Sector Compensation Strategy

Public organizations compete for talent differently from private firms. They often cannot match private cash, but they offer a different bundle: stronger pensions, healthcare, job security, and predictable advancement, traded for lower variable pay and slower market adjustment. That bundle shapes a different employment relationship, oriented toward long-term retention, stability, and public accountability rather than rapid upside. Public pay also operates under greater transparency, political scrutiny, and legal constraint, as Chapter 3 details for California. The strategic task is the same as anywhere, fit pay to the mission, but the levers differ: a public employer competes on security, purpose, and structure more than on the size of the check. Exhibit 2.3 summarizes the contrast.

Exhibit 2.3 · Public- vs. Private-Sector Compensation Strategy

Public Sector	Private Sector
Greater structure and consistency	Greater managerial flexibility
Strong pensions and benefits	Greater variable and incentive pay
Higher transparency by law	More discretion and confidentiality
Longer-term retention focus	Faster market-based adjustment
Political and public accountability	Competitive-market pressure

Exhibit 2.3 · Public- and private-sector compensation strategies emphasize different levers.

ETHICS LENS · WHEN STRATEGY REWARDS THE WRONG BEHAVIOR

Compensation strategies fail most often not because incentives are too weak but because they reward a narrow outcome while ignoring its side effects: aggressive sales targets that invite cutting corners, productivity bonuses that erode quality, individual awards that quietly punish teamwork, short-term incentives that discourage long-term investment. Designing a strategy therefore means balancing performance against ethics, sustainability, and culture, and asking not only what a plan will reward, but what it will reward at the expense of.

Conclusion: Three Takeaways

First, there is no one-size-fits-all compensation strategy; best practices matter for the technical basics, but best fit is where an organization competes, so strategy must map to mission, workforce, and context. Second, remember AMO: pay alone will never solve a performance problem, because ability and opportunity must be in place before compensation can do its work. Third, every compensation strategy should pass three tests, alignment, differentiation, and value; if it fails any one of them, redesign before you implement.

A compensation strategy establishes what an organization wants to reward. The chapters that follow examine how it translates that strategy into practice: internal alignment and job structure (Chapter 4), market pricing against the outside world (Chapter 5), and the administration of base pay (Chapter 6).

Key Terms

The following terms, set in bold throughout the chapter, anchor the framework.

Term	Definition
Compensation strategy	A coherent set of pay decisions that supports how an organization competes and wins.
Best practices	Designing pay by copying what successful organizations do; best for the technical basics.
Best fit	Designing pay for an organization's own strategy, workforce, context, and mission.
Compensation philosophy	A short, formal statement of how an organization intends to pay, what it values, and how pay supports strategy.
Skills-based pay	Paying for demonstrated skills, competencies, and certifications rather than for job title or tenure.
Compensation strategy matrix	A tool mapping organizational strategies (cost, innovation, service, public service, growth) to the pay characteristics that fit each.
Skills-based pay	Basing pay on the specific, market-valued capabilities a person holds rather than on job title alone.
Agency theory	The view that owners must design pay so agents' self-interest aligns with the owners' interests.
Expectancy theory	The view that effort depends on believing effort yields performance, performance yields reward, and the reward is valued.
Human capital theory	The view that pay reflects the value of, and investment in, a person's skills and knowledge.
AMO	Performance as the product of Ability, Motivation, and Opportunity; any one at zero yields zero.
Pay for performance	Linking reward to measured results so that pay rises and falls with performance.
Equity compensation	Stock-based pay (such as RSUs or options) that ties employees to long-run firm value; in private firms it may stay illiquid until a liquidity event.

Term	Definition
Alignment test	Does the strategy fit the mission and the rest of the organization's strategy?
Differentiation test	Does the approach distinguish the organization where distinction matters?
Value test	Does the result justify the cost (turnover, productivity, compliance)?
Lead / lag / match	Paying above, below, or at market, chosen role by role.
Line of sight	The clarity with which an employee can see how their effort affects their pay.
Vicious / virtuous circle	A self-reinforcing cycle that compensation design can worsen or break.

Discussion Questions

1. Choose one organization (public, private, or nonprofit) and walk its compensation strategy through the four steps: assess, choose, implement, reassess.
2. Propose one specific change to that organization's pay design and defend it using the three tests: alignment, differentiation, and value.
3. Is the organization closer to best fit or best practices today, and where should it be? Explain.
4. Using the AMO equation, describe a time when pay failed to fix a performance problem, and identify which term was the real constraint.
5. The school-district vicious circle persisted while the FAA broke its cycle. What made the difference, and is the FAA's approach replicable in education or public safety?
6. How should the LAPD respond strategically to a federal competitor offering $50,000 signing bonuses, given that it cannot simply outbid on cash?
7. Tesla ties almost all of Musk's reward to extreme market-capitalization and operational milestones. Use agency theory and the three tests to argue whether this is sound compensation strategy or a governance failure.
8. Compare Databricks' use of illiquid equity plus tender offers with Oracle's founder equity. What does each reveal about when equity is the right compensation strategy, and what are its risks?
9. Some organizations are shifting from paying for job titles to paying for scarce skills. Choose a role you know, identify a skill that might warrant a premium, and describe the guardrails you would set so the premium does not undermine internal equity.

Applied Case · Three Roles, One Budget

A California transit agency must set a compensation strategy for three roles under a tight budget: a bus operator (a unionized, high-turnover role the agency struggles to keep staffed), a data analyst (a scarce skill it competes for against private tech firms), and a long-range planner (a mission-driven role with few outside substitutes). A new private logistics employer has just opened nearby and is hiring operators and analysts aggressively. As the agency's compensation analyst, recommend a strategy for the three roles.

Case questions

1. Apply the four-step process. What would the Assess step reveal about each role's labor market?
2. Choose a lead, lag, or match posture for each of the three roles and justify it.
3. Which non-cash levers (pension, schedule, mission, development) would you use for the roles you cannot afford to lead on?
4. Run your overall recommendation through the three tests and note where it is weakest.

References

ABC7 Los Angeles. (2023). LAUSD, teachers union reach tentative labor agreement; and coverage of the 2023 LAPD contract. https://abc7.com/lapd-contract-pay-increase-karen-bass/13583117/

Adams, J. S. (1965). Inequity in social exchange. In L. Berkowitz (Ed.), Advances in experimental social psychology (Vol. 2, pp. 267-299). Academic Press.

Appelbaum, E., Bailey, T., Berg, P., & Kalleberg, A. L. (2000). Manufacturing advantage: Why high-performance work systems pay off. Cornell University Press.

Babcock, L., & Laschever, S. (2003). Women don't ask: Negotiation and the gender divide. Princeton University Press.

Becker, G. S. (1964). Human capital: A theoretical and empirical analysis. University of Chicago Press.

California Globe. (2023). LA schools, teachers union agree to 21% pay raise in three-year contract. https://californiaglobe.com/fr/la-schools-teachers-union-agree-to-21-pay-raise-in-three-year-contract/

CNBC. (2025a). Tesla shareholders approve Musk's $1 trillion pay plan. https://www.cnbc.com/2025/11/06/tesla-shareholders-musk-pay.html

CNBC. (2025b). Databricks raises capital at $134 billion valuation in latest funding round. https://www.cnbc.com/2025/12/16/databricks-funding-valuation.html

DiMaggio, P. J., & Powell, W. W. (1983). The iron cage revisited: Institutional isomorphism and collective rationality in organizational fields. American Sociological Review, 48(2), 147-160.

Doerr, J. (2018). Measure what matters: How Google, Bono, and the Gates Foundation rock the world with OKRs. Portfolio.

EdSource. (2026). LAUSD approves reduction in force that could affect 3,200 employees. https://edsource.org/2026/los-angeles-unified-votes-to-lay-off-3200-employees-due-to-budget-deficit/751490

Electrek. (2025). Delaware court reinstates Musk's $55B pay package, penalizes him $1 instead. https://electrek.co/2025/12/20/delaware-court-reinstates-musks-55b-pay-package-penalizes-him-1-instead/

FactCheck.org. (2026). ICE officers and bonuses. https://www.factcheck.org/2026/02/ice-officers-and-bonuses/

Federal Aviation Administration. (2025). Air traffic controller workforce plan 2025-2028. https://www.faa.gov/about/office_org/headquarters_offices/afn/offices/finance/offices/office-financial-labor-analysis/plans/controller-workforce.pdf

Fortune. (2025). Larry Ellison surpasses Elon Musk as world's richest person after Oracle's stock surge. https://fortune.com/2025/09/10/larry-ellison-elon-musk-oracle-stock-worlds-richest-person/

Jensen, M. C., & Meckling, W. H. (1976). Theory of the firm: Managerial behavior, agency costs and ownership structure. Journal of Financial Economics, 3(4), 305-360.

Lafley, A. G., & Charan, R. (2008). The game-changer: How you can drive revenue and profit growth with innovation. Crown Business.

Lafley, A. G., & Martin, R. L. (2013). Playing to win: How strategy really works. Harvard Business Review Press.

LAist. (2023). LAUSD reaches deal with support staff on salary increases, other benefits, after three-day strike ends. https://laist.com/news/education/lausd-seiu-local-99-reach-tentative-deal-following-three-day-strike

Lazear, E. P., & Rosen, S. (1981). Rank-order tournaments as optimum labor contracts. Journal of Political Economy, 89(5), 841-864.

NBC News. (2025). ICE is leaning hard on recruitment, but immigration experts say that could come at a price. https://www.nbcnews.com/news/us-news/ice-recruitment-dean-cain-signing-bonus-noem-immigration-rcna223463

Sinek, S. (2019). The infinite game. Portfolio.

U.S. Department of Transportation. (2025). Transportation Secretary Sean P. Duffy hits air traffic controller hiring goal for FY25. https://www.transportation.gov/briefing-room/trumps-transportation-secretary-sean-p-duffy-hits-air-traffic-controller-hiring-goal

U.S. Government Accountability Office. (2026). Air traffic control workforce: FAA should establish goals and better assess its hiring processes (GAO-26-107320). https://files.gao.gov/reports/GAO-26-107320/index.html

Vroom, V. H. (1964). Work and motivation. Wiley.

COMPENSATION: REWARDING AND RETAINING TALENT · CALIFORNIA EDITION
CHAPTER 3

Chapter 3. The California Compensation Environment

Why a pay system that is lawful elsewhere can be unlawful here.

Thomas J. Norman, Ph.D.

Photograph by Thomas J. Norman

OPENING CASE · WHEN "LAWFUL ELSEWHERE" MEETS CALIFORNIA

A growing software company headquartered in Texas opened its first California office. Its hiring playbook had always worked: post the role without a salary figure, ask each applicant for their current pay to 'stay competitive,' and classify the new engineers as salaried and exempt at $60,000 a year. In Texas, none of that drew a second look.

In California, all three steps were problems. The posting violated the state's pay-scale disclosure rule, the salary-history question is prohibited, and a $60,000 'exempt' salary fell below California's 2026 floor of $70,304, so those engineers were owed overtime. Within a month the company faced an applicant complaint and an annual pay-data report it had never prepared.

Nothing about the company's intentions had changed. It had simply crossed into one of the most regulated compensation environments in the country, where the law shapes reward design before strategy ever enters the room.

Learning Objectives

After studying this chapter, you should be able to do the following:

1. Summarize the major California legal and policy issues that affect compensation.
2. Explain how pay transparency and equal-pay rules influence reward design.
3. Identify the most common compliance risks in California compensation systems.
4. Discuss how California-specific rules alter compensation strategy.
5. Explain how California's agriculture and entertainment industries illustrate both the reach and the limits of compensation law.

Why California Is Different

California consistently sets higher pay floors and stronger transparency and equity rules than federal law. For a compensation manager, that means the legal environment is not a side task handled after the strategy is built; it is part of the strategy itself. The rules shape what an employer may ask, what it must disclose, how it must justify pay differences, and what it must report to the state. This chapter maps that landscape, and the practical lesson runs through all of it: in California, the law sets the boundaries inside which every reward decision is made.

Wage-and-Hour Floors

The first thing California law fixes is the bottom of the structure. Effective January 1, 2026, the statewide minimum wage is $16.90 per hour for employers of every size, and many cities set local minimums higher still. Two industries carry their own higher floors: covered fast-food restaurant workers earn at least $20.00 per hour under Assembly Bill 1228, and covered health-care workers earn between roughly $23 and $25 per hour under Senate Bill 525, depending on the type and size of the facility, with the higher rates phasing in through 2026 and beyond.

California law also draws the line between salaried and hourly work higher than federal law does. To classify a white-collar employee as exempt from overtime, an employer must pay at least twice the state minimum wage for full-time work, which in 2026 is $70,304 per year, and the employee must actually perform exempt duties more than half the time. Special rates apply to certain roles, such as $58.85 per hour for the computer-software exemption and $107.17 per hour for licensed physicians. The federal comparisons are far lower: a $7.25 minimum wage and a $35,568 exempt-salary threshold. An employer that meets the federal rules can still violate California's.

California Spotlight: Long Beach and the Olympic Wage

Long Beach is the city that organizes itself around the question of who works in it. The Port of Long Beach handles roughly forty percent of the containerized goods entering the United States, the city's hotels and restaurants will host visitors during the 2028 Summer Olympics, and an unusually large share of its workforce is unionized across sectors. Under Mayor Rex Richardson, a Cal State Dominguez Hills alumnus elected the first Black mayor of Long Beach in November 2022, the city has used the run-up to the Olympics to put two voter-approved compensation measures on the ground.

Measure RW, approved by voters in March 2024, established what was at the time the highest hotel-worker minimum wage in the United States. The measure applies to Long Beach hotels with one hundred or more rooms. Wages rose to $23 per hour as of July 20, 2024 — a thirty-one percent jump over the prior city minimum for affected workers — and escalate at six and one-half percent per year, reaching approximately $29.50 per hour by the 2028 Olympics (LAANE, 2024). The City of Los Angeles followed with a parallel ordinance for hotels with sixty or more rooms and for airport workers, scheduled to reach $25 in July 2026, $27.50 in July 2027, and $30 by July 2028 (CDF Labor Law, 2025).

Measure JB, approved in November 2024, took a different approach to the same broader question. Rather than setting a citywide pay floor for a single industry, Measure JB modernized Long Beach's civil-service hiring system to expand access to public-sector union jobs — a structural intervention designed to make a working-class career path into city employment more navigable, on the theory that quality public-sector jobs are themselves a regional wage floor for adjacent industries.

The pattern across Long Beach city-employee bargaining units illustrates how voter-approved measures interact with collective bargaining. For fiscal years 2025–2028, the firefighters' association settled at general increases of two, three, and four percent across the three years; the police officers' association settled at three, four, and five percent; the International Association of Machinists settled at one and one-quarter percent in the first year (City of Long Beach, 2025). The City's nine recognized employee organizations cover twenty-three bargaining units and roughly five thousand employees. The structural lesson is that an Olympic-wage policy targets a narrow industry, while collective bargaining sets the pay structure for the city's own workforce; both layers together — plus civil-service reform — make up the rate sheet of a working California city.

The teaching point for students is that California compensation policy is increasingly local. Cities are no longer waiting for state action; they are using direct-democracy measures, civil-service reform, and large-event leverage like the Olympics to set ambitious pay floors for industries they care about. For compensation managers operating in Los Angeles County, the implication is that a single state-level minimum wage no longer describes the floor that matters; the city-by-city patchwork does.

Pay Transparency and the Salary-History Ban

California has moved aggressively toward openness about pay. Under **Senate Bill 1162** (effective 2023), employers with fifteen or more employees generally must include the pay scale in any job posting, and any current employee may request the pay scale for their own position. Employers must also keep records of job titles and wage histories. Separately, the state's **salary-history ban** (Labor Code section 432.3, in force since 2018) prohibits asking applicants about their pay history; an employer may ask about salary expectations but must set offers on the role's value and the candidate's qualifications. Together, these rules push employers to define pay ranges deliberately and to defend them with evidence, because the ranges are now visible to applicants, employees, and regulators.

Then and Now: SB 1162 in Practice

California's Senate Bill 1162 took effect on January 1, 2023, after enactment in 2022. Employers with fifteen or more employees became required to include pay scales in job postings, and employers with one hundred or more employees became required to file annual pay data reports with the California Civil Rights Department detailing wages by race, ethnicity, and gender for each job category. Penalties for non-compliance range up to $10,000 per violation for missing pay ranges in job postings and up to $1,000 per employee for repeated pay data report failures (California Civil Rights Department, 2026).

The visible effects appeared quickly. A 2024 California Civil Rights Department survey reported that roughly seventy percent of applicants now skip job postings that omit salary ranges, and firms that complied early reported faster recruitment cycles and fewer declined offers (California Civil Rights Department, 2024). Enforcement followed compliance. The Civil Rights Department began sending warning letters and litigating against non-filers, with Cambrian Homecare settling for approximately $100,000 in 2024 and a large retailer paying six-figure penalties before its data was accepted.

The San Francisco Bay Area technology sector has been a particularly visible laboratory for the law. Tech companies with multi-location operations and remote workers face the complexity of disclosing range information across labor markets that vary widely in cost of living. Some companies posted ranges so wide that the disclosure conveyed little real information, and the Civil Rights Department's enforcement guidance has gradually tightened around what counts as a good-faith pay scale. The broader effect inside compensation departments has been to accelerate the work of internal-equity audits, range-construction discipline, and market-data verification — practices that ought to have been routine in any case but that the law now requires organizations to defend in public.

The teaching point is that pay transparency does not so much create new compensation obligations as expose existing ones. Internal inequities that were always there become visible. Range structures that were always loose have to tighten. The disclosure rule, in other words, is a forcing function for the disciplines this textbook has been arguing for all along. Chapter 5 returns to the market-pricing implications, Chapter 6 to the structure-construction implications, and Chapter 9 returns to the broader question of how compensation strategy evolves in industries — like Bay Area technology — where stock options have already made many employees wealthy and pay alone is no longer the principal motivator.

California Spotlight: The City of Bell Scandal and the Public-Pay Database

Where SB 1162 forced pay transparency on private employers, the predicate for public-employee transparency in California was the 2010 scandal in the City of Bell. Bell is a small Los Angeles County city of approximately thirty-six thousand residents and a median household income of about thirty thousand dollars. In July 2010 the Los Angeles Times reported, after investigation, that the city's Chief Administrative Officer, Robert Rizzo, had constructed a compensation package that paid him a base salary of approximately $787,000 with twelve percent annual increases scheduled every July, reaching roughly $1.5 million in his final year. The chief of police was paid approximately $457,000, the assistant chief administrative officer approximately $336,000, and the part-time city council members approximately $100,000 each (Los Angeles Times, 2010).

Rizzo was eventually convicted on fifty-three counts and sentenced to twelve years in federal prison, with separate federal tax-evasion charges adding thirty-three months. Six other Bell city officials, including the mayor, were convicted in related corruption cases (NPR, 2014; U.S. Department of Justice, 2016).

The structural response was a public database. In the aftermath of the scandal, the California State Controller built Government Compensation in California (publicpay.ca.gov), a comprehensive public-facing system that posts pay and benefit information for every employee in the state's cities, counties, special districts, state agencies, courts, K–12 districts, the University of California, the California State University, and California Community Colleges. The database is updated annually and is the principal mechanism by which California citizens can verify whether the public is being charged a defensible price for the labor it hires (California State Controller, n.d.).

The teaching point for students is the obverse of the SB 1162 lesson. SB 1162 exposed private-sector compensation by forcing job-posting disclosure; the Bell scandal exposed public-sector compensation by forcing line-item annual reporting. In both cases the disclosure rule did not create the underlying problem; it created the visibility that turned the problem into a political and legal liability. For students working in or around California public agencies, the implication is direct: every salary they design will be publicly searchable within a year of being paid.

Equal Pay

The California Equal Pay Act (Labor Code section 1197.5) is among the strongest in the nation. It requires equal pay for substantially similar work, judged by a composite of skill, effort, and responsibility performed under similar working conditions. An employer may justify a pay difference only through bona fide factors such as a seniority system, a merit system, a system that measures earnings by quantity or quality of production, or another bona fide factor like education, training, or experience, and the factor must be applied reasonably and account for the entire difference. Critically, an applicant's prior salary cannot, by itself, justify a disparity, which is one reason the salary-history ban and the Equal Pay Act work together.

Pay Data Reporting

Larger employers must also show their work. Private employers with 100 or more payroll employees, and those with 100 or more workers hired through labor contractors, must file an annual pay data report with the California Civil Rights Department, reporting pay and hours by job category, sex, race, and ethnicity across defined pay bands. The reports for the 2025 reporting year are due in mid-May 2026. The requirement does more than generate a filing: it pressures organizations to review their pay structures systematically and to notice disparities before a regulator does.

Prevailing Wage and the Public Sector

In the public sector, two further features shape pay. On most public-works projects, California requires contractors to pay the prevailing wage for each craft, set by the Department of Industrial Relations, so portions of a public pay structure are fixed by law before any internal judgment is made. And public salaries are public record, searchable through resources such as the State Controller's Government Compensation in California database. Combined with civil-service classification, this transparency makes internal alignment in government a continuous public conversation, and it raises the premium on procedural fairness.

Two California Worlds of Work: Fields and Studios

California's compensation environment is not only a set of statutes; it lives in industries found at this scale almost nowhere else. Two of them, agriculture in the Central Valley and entertainment in Los Angeles, show how the state's rules, unions, and labor markets reshape pay in ways a national playbook never anticipates.

The Fields: Agriculture and the Overtime Paradox

California is the nation's largest agricultural producer, and its hundreds of thousands of farmworkers, many of them immigrants, were for decades excluded from basic wage protections. Assembly Bill 1066 (2016) changed that, phasing in overtime until, on January 1, 2025, every California farm employer, regardless of size, had to pay overtime after eight hours in a day or forty in a week, with double time beyond twelve, the same standard other industries follow (California Department of Industrial Relations, 2025).

The result is a cautionary compensation lesson. Because growers of globally traded crops cannot simply raise prices to cover higher labor costs, many responded by capping hours at forty to avoid the overtime premium. Workers who had earned more by working fifty or sixty hours saw their weekly take-home pay fall, by roughly one hundred dollars a week in one analysis, even as their hourly protection improved (Cornell Agricultural Workforce Development, 2024). A rule written to help the lowest-paid workers shows how compensation operates inside hard market constraints: when an employer cannot pass costs through, a mandated premium can turn into fewer hours rather than more pay. Piece-rate pay (governed by Assembly Bill 1513, which requires separate pay for rest breaks and nonproductive time), the federal H-2A guest-worker wage, and the collective-bargaining structure of the United Farm Workers under California's Agricultural Labor Relations Act add still more layers found in no other low-wage sector. For a compensation manager, the fields illustrate the chapter's theme in its starkest form: the law sets a floor, but markets, hours, and immigration policy determine what workers actually earn.

Then and Now: AB 1066 — The Agricultural Overtime Phase-In Complete

Assembly Bill 1066 (2016) phased agricultural workers in California into overtime parity with workers in most other industries. The phase-in began in 2019 for large employers (twenty-six or more employees) and was completed on January 1, 2025, when employers with twenty-five or fewer employees became fully subject to overtime pay after eight hours per day and forty hours per week (California Department of Industrial Relations, n.d.; California Legislative Information, 2016).

The policy was straightforward and the moral case for it was strong. Agricultural workers had been the principal exception to California’s general daily-overtime rule, and the federal Fair Labor Standards Act still exempts them from overtime entirely. AB 1066 brought California’s farmworkers to parity with other workers in the state. The empirical results, however, complicate the policy story.

Research conducted at the University of California and Cornell using the National Agricultural Workers Survey found that during the first two years of phased implementation, the share of farmworkers working more than fifty hours per week — the original overtime threshold — dropped by approximately half. Average weekly earnings fell by about $100 per worker. The share of the workforce earning at the upper and middle tiers each declined by roughly a third. Across the affected workforce, the law was associated with a loss of approximately 15,000 to 45,000 hours and $6 million to $9 million in earnings in the first two years (Hill, 2024). The mechanism was uncomfortable but mechanical. Employers facing higher hourly costs limited most workers to forty hours per week rather than pay time-and-a-half.

The teaching point is both legal and economic. Pay structure is not policy-neutral. A change to the daily and weekly overtime thresholds, designed to raise worker earnings, produced the opposite effect for a substantial portion of the affected workforce, because employers held weekly hours below the overtime threshold rather than pay overtime. The structural lesson is that legislatures and reformers cannot fully control the response curve of the employer side. For students designing or evaluating California-specific compensation policy, the AB 1066 evidence is a useful caution against the assumption that a policy and its intended outcome are the same thing.

The Studios: Unions, Residuals, and the AI Question

Two hundred miles south, Los Angeles anchors an entertainment industry whose pay practices look like nothing else in the economy. Work is project-based and heavily unionized, through the Writers Guild of America, SAG-AFTRA, the Directors Guild, and IATSE, and a signature feature is the residual, a payment made each time a film or show is reused or streamed, so compensation continues long after the work is finished.

In 2023 those pay structures collided with streaming and artificial intelligence. After strikes lasting 148 days for writers and 118 days for actors, the guilds won higher minimums, a new streaming-success residual that pays a bonus when a title draws a large share of a service's subscribers within its first ninety days, and landmark AI protections: studios must obtain consent and pay for digital replicas of performers, and AI cannot be used to strip writers of credit or compensation (Deadline, 2023). The fight previewed a question every compensation system will eventually face, namely how to value, and protect, human work that a machine can imitate.

The industry has also been reshaped by the #MeToo movement, which since 2017 has driven new working-condition standards, from intimacy coordinators on set to renewed scrutiny of gender pay gaps that once let a male co-star earn many times what a female counterpart received for the same reshoot. And in a smaller but telling change, the Academy awarded its first Oscar for casting in 2026, recognizing a craft long excluded from the profession's highest honors, a reminder that recognition itself, not only cash, is part of how a field rewards its people (Backstage, 2024). For a compensation manager, the studios show the other end of California's range: a market where unions set the rules, where pay can outlive the job through residuals, and where technology and culture are rewriting what counts as fair pay faster than statutes can keep up.

Gig Work and Worker Classification

No question in California compensation is more consequential than a deceptively simple one: is a worker an employee or an independent contractor? The answer decides whether minimum wage, overtime, meal and rest breaks, workers' compensation, unemployment insurance, and nearly every protection described in this chapter apply at all. Misclassification does not merely shift paperwork; it removes a worker from almost the entire compensation system.

For most of the state's history the test was loose. That changed in 2018, when the California Supreme Court in Dynamex Operations West v. Superior Court adopted the strict "ABC test," which the Legislature then codified in Assembly Bill 5 (2019). Under the ABC test, a worker is presumed to be an employee unless the hiring entity can prove all three conditions: (A) the worker is free from the company's control and direction; (B) the work falls outside the company's usual course of business; and (C) the worker is customarily engaged in an independently established trade. Because prong B is hard to meet for anyone doing the company's core work, AB 5 reclassified large parts of the workforce as employees.

The fiercest reaction came from the app-based economy, whose entire model rested on contractor drivers. Facing existential cost increases, Uber, Lyft, DoorDash, and Instacart backed Proposition 22, which California voters approved in November 2020. Prop 22 carves app-based rideshare and delivery drivers out of AB 5: they remain independent contractors but receive a limited set of guarantees, including an earnings floor tied to engaged time and a health-care stipend for those who drive enough hours. After years of litigation, the California Supreme Court unanimously upheld Proposition 22 in July 2024 in Castellanos v. State of California, settling, at least for now, that the carve-out is constitutional (Perkins Coie, 2024).

For a compensation manager the lesson is structural. Classification is the threshold decision on which every other compensation choice depends, and in California it is both strictly defined and vigorously enforced, with steep penalties for getting it wrong. The gig saga also shows that classification is no longer a purely legal question; it is strategic and political, contested in courtrooms and at the ballot box, and still evolving.

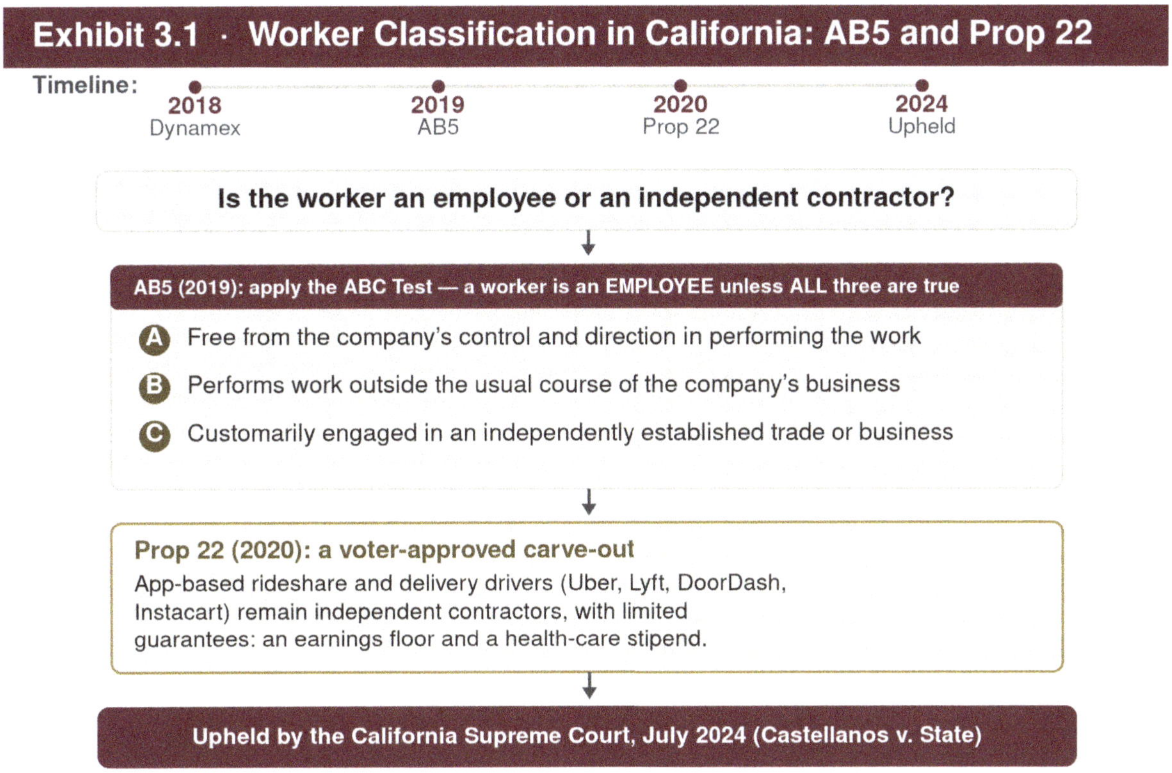

Exhibit 3.1 · Worker classification in California: the ABC test (AB 5) and the Prop 22 carve-out.

Turning Compliance into Strategy

It is tempting to treat all of this as a compliance burden, a list of rules to satisfy and move on. The better view is that California's rules push organizations toward exactly the discipline that good compensation requires: a clear pay philosophy, defensible ranges, documented job content, and structures that can withstand scrutiny. In the language of the DART model, transparency and equal-pay rules raise the bar on Assessment and Attraction, because ranges must be deliberate and defensible, and on Rewarding and Retaining, because structures must be equitable and explainable. Handled well, compliance is not a tax on strategy; it is a forcing function for a better one.

Exhibit 3.2 · California at a Glance (2026)

Item	California (2026)	Federal (for contrast)
State minimum wage	$16.90 / hour	$7.25 / hour
Exempt white-collar salary	$70,304 / year ($1,352 / week)	$35,568 / year ($684 / week)
Computer-software exemption	$58.85 / hour	(no separate rate)
Licensed physician exemption	$107.17 / hour	(no separate rate)

Item	California (2026)	Federal (for contrast)
Fast-food minimum wage (AB 1228)	$20.00 / hour	(none)
Health-care worker wage (SB 525)	~$23-$25 / hour by facility	(none)
Pay scale in job postings (SB 1162)	Employers with 15+ employees	(no federal rule)
Pay data reporting (to CRD)	Employers with 100+ employees	(no federal rule)

Note. *Figures are current for 2026 and change with annual adjustments and new legislation; verify against the Department of Industrial Relations and the Civil Rights Department before relying on them.*

Key Terms

Term	Definition
Minimum wage	The lowest hourly wage an employer may pay; in California, $16.90 statewide in 2026, with higher local and industry rates.
Exempt employee	An employee who meets a duties test and a salary threshold ($70,304 in California in 2026) and is therefore exempt from overtime.
Pay transparency (SB 1162)	California's requirement that employers with 15+ employees post pay scales and disclose them to employees on request.
Salary-history ban	Labor Code section 432.3, which prohibits asking applicants about their pay history.
California Equal Pay Act	Labor Code section 1197.5, requiring equal pay for substantially similar work and limiting the defenses an employer may raise.
Pay data reporting	The annual report of pay and demographics that employers with 100+ employees must file with the California Civil Rights Department.
Prevailing wage	A legally required wage rate for each craft on public-works projects, set by the Department of Industrial Relations.
Sectoral minimum wage	An industry-specific floor above the statewide minimum, such as the fast-food (AB 1228) and health-care (SB 525) rates.
Agricultural overtime (AB 1066)	California's phased rule, fully effective in 2025, requiring farm employers of all sizes to pay overtime after 8 hours a day or 40 a week.
Residual	A payment to writers, actors, and others each time a film or show is reused, rerun, or streamed, so pay continues after the work is done.
Independent contractor	A worker in an independently established trade who is not an employee and to whom most wage-and-hour protections do not apply.
ABC test	The standard from Dynamex (2018), codified by AB 5, under which a worker is an employee unless the hiring entity proves all three of prongs A, B, and C.
Proposition 22	The 2020 ballot measure, upheld by the California Supreme Court in 2024, classifying app-based rideshare and delivery drivers as independent contractors with limited guaranteed benefits.

Discussion Questions

1. Return to the opening case. Identify each California rule the company violated and the simplest fix for each, then explain which fix is hardest to make and why.
2. How do the salary-history ban and the Equal Pay Act reinforce each other? What would change if only one of them existed?
3. California's pay-scale posting rule makes ranges visible to current employees. How might that visibility change the way managers set and explain raises?
4. Is pay-data reporting a compliance burden, a strategic tool, or both? Defend your answer with a specific example.
5. Choose an industry with its own California floor (fast food or health care). How does a sectoral minimum wage reshape an employer's internal pay structure above that floor?
6. California's farm-overtime law (AB 1066) was meant to help the lowest-paid workers, yet some saw weekly earnings fall. Using the idea of market constraints, explain how a worker-protective law can reduce take-home pay, and what an employer might do about it.
7. Residuals and the 2023 AI provisions show entertainment unions shaping pay around how work is reused and replicated. What can an employer outside entertainment learn from how those contracts value and protect human work?

Applied Case · The Pay-Data Report That Found a Gap

Harborview Health, a California nonprofit with 240 employees, filed its annual pay data report for the first time after crossing the 100-employee threshold. Compiling the report, the HR director noticed that two job categories doing substantially similar coordination work, one historically filled mostly by women and one mostly by men, sat in different pay bands by an average of nine percent. No one had set out to pay them differently; the gap had accumulated over years of individual offers, several of them anchored to applicants' prior salaries before the practice was changed.

The chief executive has asked you to recommend a response that satisfies the California Equal Pay Act, is fair to current employees, and is defensible if the Civil Rights Department asks questions.

Case questions

1. Does the nine-percent gap, by itself, violate the Equal Pay Act? What additional information would you need to know?
2. Which bona fide factors could lawfully justify part of the gap, and which clearly could not?

3. Propose a correction plan and explain how you would communicate it so that it builds trust rather than inviting more claims.
4. What ongoing process should Harborview adopt so the gap does not reopen, and how does pay-data reporting support it?

References

Backstage. (2024). *Best Casting Oscar: Everything we know about the Academy Award's new category*. https://www.backstage.com/magazine/article/best-casting-oscar-news-79618/

California Civil Rights Department. (2024). Pay transparency outcomes survey. https://calcivilrights.ca.gov/paydatareporting/

California Civil Rights Department. (2026). *Pay data reporting*. https://calcivilrights.ca.gov/paydatareporting/

California Department of Industrial Relations. (n.d.). Overtime for agricultural workers — Frequently asked questions. https://www.dir.ca.gov/dlse/Overtime-for-Agricultural-Workers-FAQ.html

California Legislative Information. (2016). AB-1066 Agricultural workers: Wages, hours, and working conditions. https://leginfo.legislature.ca.gov/faces/billNavClient.xhtml?bill_id=201520160AB1066

California State Controller. (n.d.). Government compensation in California. https://publicpay.ca.gov/

CDF Labor Law. (2025). Olympic wages approved by Los Angeles City Council. https://www.cdflaborlaw.com/blog/olympic-wages-approved-by-los-angeles-city-council

City of Long Beach. (2025). City of Long Beach reaches agreement with its largest labor union [press release]. https://www.longbeach.gov/press-releases/city-of-long-beach-reaches-agreement-with-its-largest-labor-union/

Hill, A. E. (2024). Impact of overtime on California farm worker hours and earnings. Cornell Agricultural Workforce Development. https://agworkforce.cals.cornell.edu/2024/07/17/impact-of-overtime-on-california-farm-worker-hours-and-earnings/

LAANE. (2024). Long Beach voters approve Measure RW. Los Angeles Alliance for a New Economy. https://laane.org/press_releases/long-beach-voters-approve-measure-rw/

Los Angeles Times. (2010, July 15). Is a city manager worth $800,000? https://www.latimes.com/local/la-me-bell-salary-20100715-story.html

NPR. (2014, April 16). Ex-city manager caught in Calif. salary scandal gets 12 years. https://www.npr.org/sections/thetwo-way/2014/04/16/303768753/

U.S. Department of Justice, Central District of California. (2016). Former Chief Administrative Officer for City of Bell sentenced to federal prison for cheating IRS to avoid taxes on corrupt activities. https://www.justice.gov/usao-cdca/pr/former-chief-administrative-officer-city-bell-sentenced-federal-prison-cheating-irs

California Department of Industrial Relations. (2025). *California Equal Pay Act.* https://www.dir.ca.gov/dlse/california_equal_pay_act.htm

California Department of Industrial Relations. (2025). *Minimum wage.* https://www.dir.ca.gov/dlse/minimum_wage.htm

California Department of Industrial Relations. (2025). *Fast food minimum wage (AB 1228) and health care minimum wage (SB 525).* https://www.dir.ca.gov/dlse/

California Department of Industrial Relations. (2025). *Overtime for agricultural workers, frequently asked questions (AB 1066); and piece-rate compensation (AB 1513).* https://www.dir.ca.gov/dlse/Overtime-for-Agricultural-Workers-FAQ.html

California Labor Code section 432.3 (pay scale disclosure and salary-history ban) and Senate Bill 1162 (2022).

California Assembly Bill 5 (2019), codifying the ABC test, and *Dynamex Operations West, Inc. v. Superior Court*, 4 Cal. 5th 903 (2018).

Castellanos v. State of California, S279622 (Cal. July 25, 2024) (upholding Proposition 22).

Perkins Coie. (2024). *California Supreme Court upholds Proposition 22.* https://perkinscoie.com/insights/update/california-supreme-court-upholds-proposition-22

COMPENSATION: REWARDING AND RETAINING TALENT · CALIFORNIA EDITION
CHAPTER 4

Chapter 4. Defining Internal Alignment

Why the pay gaps inside an organization matter as much as the paychecks themselves.

Thomas J. Norman, Ph.D.

Photograph by Thomas J. Norman

OPENING CASE · THE $70,000 EXPERIMENT

In 2015, Dan Price, the founder of a Seattle credit-card processing company called Gravity Payments, did something almost no executive does. He announced that every employee, every single one, would earn at least $70,000 a year, and to pay for it he cut his own salary from roughly $1 million down to the same $70,000. Overnight, the distance between the lowest-paid worker and the chief executive nearly disappeared.

The press loved it. Yet the headlines skipped the most instructive part of the story. Within months, two of the company's most experienced and highest-performing employees resigned. They did not leave because they earned less; their pay had not been cut. They left because a brand-new hire with no experience now earned almost exactly what they earned after years of building skill. To them, that felt unfair.

One company, one announcement, two opposite reactions, and both are about the same thing: the structure of pay *inside* a single organization. That structure is what this chapter calls internal alignment, and learning to see it is the first step toward managing it well.

Learning Objectives

After studying this chapter, you should be able to do the following:

1. Define internal alignment and explain why the pay relationships within an organization matter for efficiency, fairness, and compliance.
2. Identify the three building blocks of any pay structure: levels, differentials, and the criteria used to set them.
3. Explain the external and organizational forces that shape internal pay structures.
4. Compare egalitarian and hierarchical pay structures and judge when each one fits the work.
5. Apply equity theory, tournament theory, and institutional theory to real pay decisions.
6. Connect internal alignment to public-sector classification systems, including the federal General Schedule and California civil service.

What Internal Alignment Means

In the previous chapter we examined compensation strategy, the broad choices an organization makes about how it competes for and rewards talent. This chapter turns inward. It looks at something quieter than strategy but every bit as powerful: the pattern of pay differences among the jobs that sit under one roof. Why does the analyst earn more than the technician? Why is there a $40,000 gap between two people whose desks are twenty feet apart? Those gaps are rarely random. They form a structure, and that structure does real work inside the organization.

Internal alignment, sometimes called **internal equity**, refers to the pay relationships among the different jobs, skills, and competencies within a single organization. The key phrase is *within a single organization*. We are not yet comparing one employee's salary to the pay of someone doing similar work at the company across town; that comparison is external competitiveness, the subject of the next chapter. For now, we are looking inward at how the pieces relate to one another.

Internal alignment touches all three of the goals that organize the study of compensation. The first is **efficiency**: a sound structure supports the workflow and steers people toward the work the organization values most. The second is **fairness**: employees constantly compare themselves to their coworkers, and those comparisons drive effort, cooperation, and the decision to stay or leave. The third is **compliance**: the structure has to satisfy the law, from minimum-wage and overtime rules to equal-pay requirements. Get internal alignment wrong, and the organization does not merely have an accounting problem; it has a motivation problem, a retention problem, and a legal problem at the same time.

The Anatomy of a Pay Structure

Every pay structure, however simple or complex, is assembled from three decisions. Master these three and you can read almost any organization's pay system.

Levels

The first decision concerns **levels**: how many rungs the ladder should have. Some organizations build a tall hierarchy of many narrow grades; others compress everything into a few broad bands. The number of levels signals how finely the organization wishes to distinguish among jobs and how much room it wants to give people to advance without changing roles entirely.

Differentials

The second decision concerns **differentials**: how large the gaps between levels should be. Is each step up a modest increase, or does each level pay dramatically more than the one below it? The size of the differential is the organization's statement about how much it is willing to reward movement up the ladder.

Criteria

The third decision concerns the **criteria** used to set the levels. Broadly, there are two choices. A **job-based** structure pays for the job a person holds, regardless of who holds it. A **person-based** structure pays for the skills and competencies the person brings, regardless of the specific job title. Most organizations blend the two, but the emphasis matters: it determines whether employees are rewarded chiefly for occupying a position or for developing capability.

A symphony orchestra is the textbook illustration of a job-based structure: pay attaches to the chair, not the player, so a principal cellist earns more than a section cellist even when the two are equally gifted. A person-based system would do the reverse, paying two equally skilled cellists the same regardless of chair. The distinction is easy to blur, but it decides whether an organization is paying for positions or for people.

Levels, differentials, and criteria. When an employee complains about pay at work, the grievance almost always traces back to one of these three, even when the person lacks the vocabulary to name it.

Job Evaluation: Determining the Relative Value of Jobs

Internal alignment raises an obvious question: how does an organization decide that one job belongs above another in the structure? The systematic answer is job evaluation, the process of assessing the relative worth of jobs to one another. The emphasis falls on the job, not the person; job evaluation rates the work and what it requires, leaving the performance and pay of the individual who holds it to other systems.

Organizations use four main approaches, trading simplicity for precision. Ranking orders whole jobs from most to least valuable; it is fast and intuitive but subjective, workable only in small organizations where one person can hold every job in mind. Classification slots jobs into grades or classes defined in advance, the method behind the federal General Schedule and most civil-service systems, where a written grade definition tells you where a job belongs. The point-factor method, the most widely used approach in large organizations, scores each job on a set of weighted compensable factors, sums the points, and converts the total into a grade; it is more work but far more defensible, because every placement traces back to specific, documented factors. Market pricing sets a job's value directly from external survey data, the subject of the next chapter; it keeps pay competitive but, used alone, can import the market's inequities and override internal logic.

Whatever the method, the heart of job evaluation is the set of compensable factors, the dimensions an organization chooses to pay for. Common factors include skill, effort, responsibility, and working conditions, often broken into sub-factors such as education, problem-solving, decision-making authority, and physical demands. The choice of factors is itself a values statement: an organization that heavily weights decision-making authority will build a different hierarchy than one that weights physical risk or customer impact. Done with care, job evaluation gives a pay structure something the market alone cannot, an internal logic employees can see, understand, and accept as fair.

Exhibit 4.1 · Four Approaches to Job Evaluation

Whole-job, qualitative — Factor-based, quantitative

Ranking
Order whole jobs from most to least valuable.
Simple and fast; subjective, best for small organizations.

Classification
Slot jobs into predefined grades or classes by definition.
Common in government (e.g., the GS system).

Point-Factor
Score each job on compensable factors and sum the points.
Detailed and defensible; the most widely used method.

Market Pricing
Set a job's value by external market survey rates.
Market-driven; can undercut internal equity if used alone.

Compensable factors: skill · effort · responsibility · working conditions · knowledge

Exhibit 4.1 · Four approaches to job evaluation, from whole-job and qualitative to factor-based and quantitative.

Two Philosophies: Egalitarian and Hierarchical

Because the three building blocks can be combined in countless ways, organizations can land almost anywhere on a spectrum. The two ends of that spectrum are worth naming.

An **egalitarian structure** has few levels and small differentials, so pay is relatively equal across the organization. Gravity Payments, from our opening case, is an extreme version. Egalitarian structures tend to support teamwork, cooperation, and a shared sense that everyone is in it together. They fit work that is highly interdependent, where people must share knowledge rather than compete with one another. Their characteristic risk is that they offer little tangible reward for standing out, which can frustrate high performers.

A **hierarchical structure** has many levels and large differentials, with substantial rewards for moving up. These structures motivate individual achievement and signal that there is a great deal to gain by climbing. They fit work in which individual performance is easy to measure and the organization wants people striving to distinguish themselves. Their characteristic risk is that wide, visible gaps can poison teamwork and breed resentment.

Neither philosophy is right or wrong in the abstract. The question is always fit: does the structure match the work and the strategy? An egalitarian pay system inside a fiercely individual sales force will feel like a brake, and a steeply hierarchical system inside a tight, interdependent research team will feel like sand in the gears.

The Forces That Shape Structures

Where a structure lands is not a free choice made in a vacuum. It is pushed and pulled by forces from outside the organization and from within it.

External Forces

Several forces press on the structure from the outside. **Economic pressure** is the largest: basic supply and demand for labor, together with the reality that an organization cannot, for long, pay a job more than the value it adds. **Government and legal forces** matter enormously, especially in the public sector, and include minimum-wage laws, the Fair Labor Standards Act, and prevailing-wage rules that dictate pay on government contracts. **Competitor pay levels** set expectations the organization cannot ignore; if every employer in the industry pays engineers a premium, that premium will shape internal relationships whether managers like it or not. Finally, **custom and culture** establish what a society or an industry has simply come to treat as normal and legitimate. Together, these external forces draw the boundaries within which the organization makes its choices.

> **CALIFORNIA SPOTLIGHT · THE LEGAL FLOOR BENEATH EVERY STRUCTURE**
>
> Before an organization decides how steep or flat its ladder will be, the law sets the lowest rung and draws the line between salaried and hourly work. In California, both lines sit well above the federal minimums, so a structure that is lawful in another state can be unlawful here.
>
> **Minimum wage.** Effective January 1, 2026, California's statewide minimum wage is \$16.90 per hour for employers of every size, up from \$16.50 in 2025 (California Department of Industrial Relations, 2025). The federal minimum wage remains \$7.25 per hour, unchanged since 2009 (U.S. Department of Labor, 2026). Many California cities set local minimums higher still.
>
> **The salaried line.** To classify a white-collar employee as exempt from overtime, California requires a salary of at least twice the state minimum wage for full-time work. In 2026 that floor rises to \$70,304 per year (\$1,352 per week). The comparable federal threshold is far lower, \$35,568 per year (\$684 per week), after a 2024 federal rule raising it was vacated by a federal court and formally rescinded in 2026 (U.S. Department of Labor, 2026). California also sets special rates for certain roles, such as \$58.85 per hour for the computer-software exemption and \$107.17 per hour for licensed physicians in 2026.
>
> **Prevailing wage.** On most public-works projects, California requires contractors to pay the prevailing wage for each craft, set by the Department of Industrial Relations. For public managers, prevailing-wage rules mean that whole portions of a pay structure are fixed by law before any internal judgment is made.

> *The lesson for internal alignment is direct: in California the bottom of the structure and the salaried/hourly boundary are set externally, by statute, and every internal differential is built on top of that floor.*

Organizational Forces

Inside the organization, several more forces shape the structure. **Strategy** comes first: an employer competing on innovation will build a different structure than one competing on low cost. **Technology and work design** matter, because capital-intensive work staffed by a few highly skilled operators looks nothing like labor-intensive work staffed by many similar roles. **Human capital**, the skill and education the work genuinely requires, pushes differentials up or down. The organization's own **HR policies and internal labor market**, the rules governing how people enter and advance, lock patterns in over time. **Employee acceptance** is essential, because a structure that people regard as illegitimate will motivate no one, however elegant it looks on paper. And **cost** is ever-present, since every additional level and every widened differential adds up. The structure an organization ends up with is the negotiated result of all these forces meeting the choices its leaders make.

Why Differentials Change Behavior: Three Theories

Why would a pay gap actually change how people behave? Three theories offer three complementary lenses, and real pay structures usually reflect all three at once.

Equity theory holds that people compare their own ratio of contribution to reward against the ratios they observe in others (Adams, 1965). When the comparison feels unbalanced, they act to restore balance: they reduce effort, they voice complaints, or they leave. That is precisely what happened to the two experienced employees in the opening case, who measured a newcomer's reward against their own years of contribution and judged the exchange unfair.

Tournament theory holds that large differentials, especially near the top of a structure, function like the prize in a tournament (Lazear & Rosen, 1981). The bigger the jump to the next level, the harder people compete to win the promotion. The theory helps explain why chief-executive pay sits so far above the next layer of management; the gap is not only a statement about the executive's value but also an incentive aimed at everyone below who hopes to climb.

Institutional theory is the most humbling of the three. It holds that organizations often adopt structures simply because those structures are normal in their field, copying one another until a practice persists because it is the way everyone does it (DiMaggio & Powell, 1983). Much of what looks like deliberate design in a pay system is, on closer inspection, imitation.

Internal Labor Markets and Career Movement

One more concept ties the structure together: the **internal labor market** (Doeringer & Piore, 1971). Most organizations do not fill every job from the outside. Instead, they maintain **entry points**, the limited set of jobs filled from the external market, and **promotion ladders**, the defined paths that move people upward and across over time. Consider the familiar progression from analyst to senior analyst to manager. The pay structure and the promotion structure are two sides of the same coin.

This pattern is especially visible in government, where entry levels, promotion eligibility, and movement between classifications are spelled out in formal, written rules. Internal labor markets create real benefits, including stability and a genuine sense of career, yet they can also create rigidity when the rules outlast the work they were written to govern.

Deciding which jobs to build and advance inside the structure, and which to fill from the outside market or contract away entirely, is itself a strategic choice, shaped by how firm-specific, complex, and interdependent the work is (Norman, 2010).

Internal labor markets are not only a feature of offices and agencies. In California's Central Valley, the Wonderful Company, among Kern County's largest private employers with thousands of workers around Bakersfield, raised its full-time farm pay well above the legal floor, a 36 percent increase to fifteen dollars an hour at the time, later moving toward seventeen, and paired it with education, wellness, and training programs that open real ladders out of entry-level field work (The Bakersfield Californian, 2018). It is a striking case of an agricultural employer building the entry points and promotion paths usually associated with white-collar firms, and a reminder that an internal labor market is a design choice available in any industry.

When Each Structure Wins: Distributive, Procedural, and Interactional Justice

So when does each approach actually pay off? Hierarchical structures tend to win when work is largely independent, when individual contributions are easy to see and measure, and when the organization wants to reward specialized expertise and reward people for climbing. Egalitarian structures tend to win when work is highly interdependent, when cooperation and knowledge-sharing matter more than individual stardom, and when wide, visible gaps would poison the very teamwork the work requires.

Running beneath both is the question of fairness, which has three distinct parts. **Distributive justice** concerns whether the outcomes, the actual pay numbers, feel fair. **Procedural justice** concerns whether the process used to set those numbers feels fair; people will accept a surprising amount of inequality in outcomes when they believe the process behind it was transparent and even-handed. **Interactional justice** concerns how the decision is delivered, whether employees receive honest explanations and are treated with dignity and respect (Bies & Moag, 1986; Colquitt, 2001). A manager can apply a fair formula through a fair process and still destroy trust by communicating a pay decision carelessly. Even small slights land hard: one large field study found that employees who received an expected recognition gift just a few weeks late cut their effort enough to cost their employer well into six figures (Harvard Business Review, 2026). Together, procedure and interpersonal treatment often matter as much as the paycheck itself.

Internal Alignment in the Public Sector

The public sector is where internal alignment is most visible and most rule-bound, which makes it an ideal place to see the concepts of this chapter in action. The federal government runs on the **General Schedule** (GS), a system of fifteen grades, each containing ten steps. An employee's grade depends on the job, while the step depends largely on time in position and performance. State and local governments use similar step-and-grade civil-service systems. The arrangement is deliberately hierarchical across grades and fairly egalitarian within them, and it leans heavily on procedural fairness through written classifications, posted rules, and transparency.

CALIFORNIA SPOTLIGHT · READING A PUBLIC SALARY IN CALIFORNIA

California's state and local governments run on step-and-grade systems that make internal alignment unusually visible. The City of Los Angeles, the County of Los Angeles, and the State of California each publish detailed salary schedules in which a classification maps to a grade and an employee advances by steps over time.

What sets the public sector apart is transparency. Public salaries are public record. Anyone can look up what a city employee earns through resources such as the State Controller's *Government Compensation in California* database. Because the numbers are open, internal alignment in government is a continuous public conversation in a way it rarely is inside a private firm, and procedural justice, demonstrating that the process was fair, carries even more weight.

For a public manager in California, this visibility is both a discipline and a vulnerability. The discipline is that structures must be defensible in the open. The vulnerability is that every compression or inversion, discussed next, is visible to the very employees most affected by it.

Exhibit 4.2 · Internal Alignment in Practice — Selected City of Los Angeles Pay Ranges

Internal alignment is easiest to see where the numbers are public. The City of Los Angeles employs roughly 34,000 full-time workers and proposed a $14.85 billion budget for 2026-27, the largest in its history (ABC7 Los Angeles, 2026). Because the City publishes a salary range for every classification, its pay structure can be read directly. The ranges below, drawn from official City classifications and postings, show how levels and differentials operate inside four very different departments.

Department	Classification	Annual range (2025-26)	What it shows
Police (LAPD)	Police Officer I-II	$91,224-$124,236	Steps within one sworn class reward tenure and the move from Police Officer I to II.
Zoo	Animal Keeper	$57,378-$83,812	A flatter craft range; specialty and experience drive the spread.
Recreation & Parks	Park Ranger (approx.)	$51,000-$77,000	RAP devotes about 83% of its budget to salaries, a labor-intensive public service.
Library	Librarian (across grades)	$75,400-$113,600	Several Librarian grades reveal levels and differentials inside one job family.

Note. *Figures are public record and current for 2025-2026. Police, Animal Keeper, and Librarian ranges are from official City of Los Angeles classifications and postings; Park Ranger figures are third-party aggregates. Ranges change with memoranda of understanding and cost-of-living adjustments.*

When Structure Breaks: Pay Compression and Inversion

Public managers live with a recurring cautionary tale: pay compression and its more severe twin, pay inversion. **Pay compression** occurs when the gap between experienced employees and newcomers shrinks until it nearly vanishes, so that years of experience stop being rewarded. It is typically driven by slow step schedules colliding with a rising external market. **Pay inversion** is worse: new hires actually earn more than the veterans sitting beside them, usually because starting salaries had to be raised to fill vacancies.

Picture a California police department or a hospital nursing unit that must offer aggressive starting rates to fill critical vacancies, while loyal employees of ten years remain stuck on a slow step schedule. Equity theory predicts exactly what follows: morale collapses, the strongest veterans leave, and the institution loses its accumulated memory and judgment. Compression is internal misalignment in its purest and most damaging form, and it is almost always the result of ignoring the structure until it breaks.

Los Angeles lived this tension. Facing what the City Council described as a hiring and retention crisis, with sworn ranks down by more than a thousand officers in three years, the City approved a 2023 contract that raised a new recruit's starting pay by roughly 13 percent, to about $86,000, and added retention bonuses (ABC7 Los Angeles, 2023). Lifting the floor to compete for recruits was reasonable, yet it moved new hires closer to mid-career veterans who advance only a step a year, and the contract's $20,000 lateral-hire bonus exceeded its $15,000 academy bonus, an internal-alignment tension every incumbent could see, because the figures are public record.

CALIFORNIA SPOTLIGHT · COMPRESSION AND INVERSION IN THE CSU

> Pay compression and inversion are not only a public-safety or nursing problem; they reach into the university where many readers of this book study and work. In 2022 the California State University engaged the consulting firm Mercer to study faculty compensation. Mercer reported to the Board of Trustees in March 2023 and published its findings that September, examining the very problems described in this section, salary compression and inversion across faculty ranks, including professors, lecturers, coaches, counselors, and librarians, alongside how CSU pay compared with the outside market (California Faculty Association, 2023; Mercer, 2023).
>
> The study put numbers to a familiar pattern. Years of flat step movement against a rising market had narrowed, and in places reversed, the distance between long-serving faculty and recent hires.
>
> Yet it drew sharp criticism for the comparison group it chose. Mercer benchmarked CSU faculty against university systems across the country but did not include the systems closest to home and most relevant to the CSU's own labor market, the University of California and the California Community Colleges, along with high-cost peers such as the State University of New York and the City University of New York. Critics argued that leaving out these local competitors understated the true gap for faculty living in California's expensive regions (California Faculty Association, 2023).
>
> *The lesson reaches past higher education. Even a rigorous external study is only as good as the comparison group it selects, and the choice of which jobs and which competitors to include is itself a judgment with real consequences. Internal alignment and external benchmarking, the subject of the next chapter, can never be fully separated.*

Conclusion: Three Questions to Carry Forward

Internal alignment is the architecture of pay inside a single organization, built from levels, differentials, and criteria, shaped by external and organizational forces, and explained by equity, tournament, and institutional theory. It is most visible, and most consequential, in the public sector, where the numbers are open to all. Three questions are worth carrying into practice and into this week's discussion.

1. Are the pay gaps between levels in your organization something people can explain and defend, or are they a mystery?
2. Does your structure fit your work? If success requires cooperation, do your pay gaps help that cooperation or fight it?
3. When a pay gap feels unfair, who decides what fair means: the market, the manager, the union, the law, or the employees themselves?

Key Terms

The following terms, set in bold throughout the chapter, are central to understanding internal alignment.

Term	Definition
Internal alignment (internal equity)	The pay relationships among the jobs, skills, and competencies within a single organization.
Pay structure	The array of pay levels and differentials an organization uses to relate its jobs to one another.
Levels	The number of rungs, grades, or bands in a pay structure.
Differentials	The size of the pay gaps between adjacent levels in a structure.
Criteria (job- vs. person-based)	The basis for setting levels: the job a person holds (job-based) or the skills and competencies a person brings (person-based).
Egalitarian structure	A structure with few levels and small differentials that favors cooperation and interdependent work.
Hierarchical structure	A structure with many levels and large differentials that favors individual achievement and measurable work.
Equity theory	The view that people compare their contribution-to-reward ratio with others' and act to restore balance when it feels unfair (Adams, 1965).
Tournament theory	The view that large differentials near the top act as prizes that intensify competition for promotion (Lazear & Rosen, 1981).
Institutional theory	The view that organizations adopt structures by imitating what is normal in their field (DiMaggio & Powell, 1983).
Internal labor market	The system of entry points and promotion ladders by which an organization fills and advances jobs from within.
Distributive justice	Perceived fairness of pay outcomes, the actual numbers.
Procedural justice	Perceived fairness of the process used to set pay.
Interactional justice	Perceived fairness in how pay decisions are communicated: honest explanations and respectful, dignified treatment.
General Schedule (GS)	The U.S. federal pay system of 15 grades and 10 steps per grade.
Job evaluation	The systematic process of assessing the relative worth of jobs to one another, rating the work rather than the person.
Compensable factors	The dimensions an organization chooses to pay for (skill, effort, responsibility, working conditions) and uses to score jobs.

Term	Definition
Point-factor method	A job-evaluation approach that scores each job on weighted compensable factors and sums the points to set its grade.
Pay compression	The shrinking of the gap between experienced employees and newcomers until experience is barely rewarded.
Pay inversion	The condition in which new hires earn more than more experienced incumbents.
Prevailing wage	A legally required wage rate for each craft on public-works projects, set in California by the Department of Industrial Relations.

Discussion Questions

1. Return to the opening case. Using equity theory, explain why two high performers left Gravity Payments even though their pay did not fall. What would you have advised Dan Price to do differently?
2. Choose an organization you know well. Describe its pay structure in terms of levels, differentials, and criteria. Is it closer to egalitarian or hierarchical, and does that fit the work?
3. California's 2026 minimum wage ($16.90) and exempt-salary floor ($70,304) sit well above the federal levels. How might these higher legal floors compress or reshape an employer's internal differentials?
4. Study Exhibit 4.2. Compare the Police Officer and Animal Keeper ranges. What do the different range widths tell you about levels, differentials, and the work each class performs?
5. Public salaries in California are public record. How does that transparency change the way a public manager must justify pay differences compared with a private-sector manager?
6. A city must raise starting pay for nurses to fill vacancies, creating inversion against ten-year veterans. Propose a defensible plan to address the inversion, and explain how procedural justice should guide it.
7. Optional viewing. In the film Hidden Figures (2016), Dorothy Vaughan performs a supervisor's full duties without the supervisor's title or pay. Whose responsibility is it to make the pay structure catch up to the work being done, and how quickly should it happen?
8. A symphony orchestra lists dozens of distinct positions and pays its principal violinist far more than a section violinist of equal skill. Is this a job-based or a person-based structure? Apply the equity and tournament models, and state what evidence you would need to judge whether the musicians see the structure as fair.

Applied Case · The Step Schedule That Stopped Working

The City of Harbor Vista, a mid-sized California municipality, staffs its public-health division through a classic civil-service step-and-grade system. A Public Health Nurse I begins at Step 1 and advances one step each year, reaching the top of the range only after five years. For two decades, the schedule worked. New nurses earned a fair starting wage, veterans earned visibly more, and the differentials between steps told a clear story: stay, grow, and your pay will grow with you.

Then the regional labor market for nurses tightened sharply. To fill four vacancies that had sat open for months, the city's human-resources director won approval to raise the starting rate for new Public Health Nurse I hires by 18 percent. The vacancies filled within weeks. Within the same month, however, three nurses with eight to ten years of service discovered that the newcomers they were training now earned more than they did. One of the three, a respected charge nurse, requested a transfer; another began interviewing at a neighboring county. Because Harbor Vista's salaries are published in the state compensation database, the figures were not in dispute, and word traveled quickly through the division.

The city manager has asked you, as a compensation analyst, to recommend a response that is both fiscally responsible and defensible to the city council, the union, and the affected employees.

Case questions

1. Identify the problem precisely. Is Harbor Vista facing compression, inversion, or both, and how can you tell from the facts given?
2. Apply equity theory to predict the behavior of the veteran nurses if nothing is done. Which employees are most at risk of leaving, and why?
3. Draft two options to restore internal alignment, one that adjusts the step schedule and one that uses a different mechanism (for example, an experience-based equity adjustment). Note the cost and the fairness trade-offs of each.
4. Harbor Vista's pay is public record. Explain how procedural justice should shape not only the solution you choose but also how you communicate it.

References

ABC7 Los Angeles. (2023, August). *LAPD officers' starting pay would increase under agreement reached by Mayor Bass, police union.* https://abc7.com/lapd-contract-pay-increase-karen-bass/13583117/

ABC7 Los Angeles. (2026, April). *Karen Bass unveils $14.9 billion proposed budget for LA that includes no layoffs.* https://abc7.com/post/karen-bass-unveils-149-billion-proposed-budget-la-includes-no-layoffs/

Adams, J. S. (1965). Inequity in social exchange. In L. Berkowitz (Ed.), *Advances in experimental social psychology* (Vol. 2, pp. 267-299). Academic Press.

The Bakersfield Californian. (2018). *Wonderful's minimum wage boost could have wider impact on Kern's labor market.* https://www.bakersfield.com/news/wonderful-s-minimum-wage-boost-could-have-wider-impact-on/article_ab1cb2d0-04b6-11e9-bdab-03596dd14538.html

Bies, R. J., & Moag, J. S. (1986). Interactional justice: Communication criteria of fairness. In R. J. Lewicki, B. H. Sheppard, & M. H. Bazerman (Eds.), *Research on negotiation in organizations* (Vol. 1, pp. 43-55). JAI Press.

California Department of Industrial Relations. (2025, August). *Minimum wage.* https://www.dir.ca.gov/dlse/minimum_wage.htm

California Faculty Association. (2023). *CSU administrators release Mercer faculty compensation study.* https://www.calfac.org/csu-administrators-release-mercer-faculty-compensation-study/

City of Los Angeles. (2025). *Police Officer (Class 2214)* [Job classification posting]. https://lacity.gov/jobs/openings/police-officer-2214-revised-080625

City of Los Angeles. (2026). *Animal Keeper (Class 4304)* [Job classification posting]. https://lacity.gov/jobs/openings/animal-keeper-4304

City of Los Angeles. (2026). *Librarian (Class 6152)* [Class specification]. https://lacity.gov/jobs/openings/librarian-6152-d-revised-01-27-2026

City of Los Angeles, Department of Recreation and Parks. (2025). *Current budget and finance.* https://needs.parks.lacity.gov/about/recreation-and-parks-today/current-budget-and-finance/

Colquitt, J. A. (2001). On the dimensionality of organizational justice: A construct validation of a measure. *Journal of Applied Psychology, 86*(3), 386-400.

DiMaggio, P. J., & Powell, W. W. (1983). The iron cage revisited: Institutional isomorphism and collective rationality in organizational fields. *American Sociological Review, 48*(2), 147-160.

Doeringer, P. B., & Piore, M. J. (1971). *Internal labor markets and manpower analysis.* D. C. Heath.

Harvard Business Review. (2026). *Research roundup: A surprising benefit of upskilling, why goals can backfire, and more.* https://hbr.org/2026/04/research-roundup-a-surprising-benefit-of-upskilling-why-goals-can-backfire-and-more

Lazear, E. P., & Rosen, S. (1981). Rank-order tournaments as optimum labor contracts. *Journal of Political Economy, 89*(5), 841-864.

Mercer. (2023). *California State University faculty compensation study*. The California State University. https://www.calstate.edu/csu-system/faculty-staff/faculty-compensation-study

Milkovich, G. T., Newman, J. M., & Gerhart, B. (2023). *Compensation* (14th ed.). McGraw-Hill Education.

Norman, T. J. (2010). *Outsourcing human resource activities: Measuring the hidden costs and benefits*. LAP Lambert Academic Publishing.

U.S. Department of Labor, Wage and Hour Division. (2026). *Fact sheet: minimum wage, overtime, and the white-collar exemptions under the FLSA.* https://www.dol.gov/agencies/whd/flsa

COMPENSATION: REWARDING AND RETAINING TALENT · CALIFORNIA EDITION
CHAPTER 5

Chapter 5. Market Pricing and External Competitiveness

What the outside market pays, and how to position against it.

Thomas J. Norman, Ph.D.

Photograph by Thomas J. Norman

OPENING CASE · THE SURVEY THAT WAS TWO YEARS OLD

Pine County, a mid-sized California employer, could not fill its civil-engineer and public-health-nurse positions. Postings sat open for months, and the few candidates who applied took other offers. When a new analyst finally pulled the numbers, the cause was plain: the county was setting salaries from a salary survey that was almost two years old, in a market where pay for those roles had climbed sharply.

The county was not underpaying on purpose. It simply did not know what the market now paid. Its internal pay structure was sound, but it had lost touch with the outside world.

This chapter is about that outside world, the labor market, and how an organization prices its jobs against it.

Learning Objectives

After studying this chapter, you should be able to do the following:

1. Explain how salary surveys are used in compensation design.
2. Interpret market data for pay-setting decisions.
3. Compare external competitiveness with internal equity.
4. Evaluate the tradeoffs between market pay and cost control.
5. Price scarce and emerging skills using real-time market signals and disciplined premium-pay guardrails.

From Inside to Outside

Chapter 4 built an internal structure: it ranked jobs by their worth to the organization. But internal value is only half the story. An employer also competes for people in a labor market, and that market has its own prices. **External competitiveness** is the pay relationship between an organization and the other employers that compete for the same talent. Where internal alignment asks how an organization's jobs relate to one another, external competitiveness asks how its pay compares with everyone else's. Both questions must be answered, and they do not always give the same answer.

The foundation under the whole of market pricing is the principle Alfred Marshall (1890) named in his Principles of Economics: labor is a derived demand. Employers do not value labor in itself; they value labor because of what labor produces. The price an employer is willing to pay for an hour of work is therefore bounded above by the marginal contribution that hour makes to the value of the output the employer sells, and bounded below by what the employee's next-best alternative employer would pay for that same hour. Marshall's four rules of derived demand — labor demand is more elastic when the final product's demand is more elastic, when other inputs can substitute for labor, when the supply of those substitutes is more elastic, and when labor costs are a large share of total cost — explain why some occupations face wage volatility that others do not (Ehrenberg & Smith, 2021). For a compensation manager, the practical implication is that market pricing is not free-floating. The market wage for any given role is the equilibrium between what employers can productively pay and what comparable employers in the relevant labor market are paying. Pay below that equilibrium and the role goes unfilled; pay above it and the employer absorbs costs that the output cannot support.

Salary Surveys

The market speaks through **salary surveys**, organized collections of pay data for defined jobs in defined markets. Surveys come from several sources: published commercial surveys, industry and professional associations, government data such as the Bureau of Labor Statistics' Occupational Employment and Wage Statistics, and, in the public sector, open databases such as the State Controller's Government Compensation in California. Some large employers also run custom surveys among a chosen set of comparators.

Good survey data shares four qualities: it covers the relevant market, it is recent, it rests on a sufficient sample, and it matches real jobs rather than titles alone. Because pay keeps moving, survey data must also be aged, or trended forward, to the date the pay will actually take effect. Numbers gathered a year ago understate this year's market, which is precisely how Pine County fell behind.

> **FROM THE FIELD · A PHOTOGRAPH OF A MOVING TARGET**
> When I worked in Silicon Valley in the late 1990s, the market moved so fast that we re-checked our survey data far more often than once a year. Today, with generative AI reshaping whole job families, that pace has only increased. A salary survey is a photograph of a moving target, and the older the photograph, the less it tells you about where the target is now.

Defining the Relevant Market

Before reading any survey, an organization must decide whose pay actually competes with its own. The relevant labor market is defined by occupation, industry, geography, and employer size, and the right comparators differ by role. A city competes with other public agencies for some jobs but with private firms for others. A civil engineer in Los Angeles can take a job at a private design firm, so the city must watch private pay; a tax auditor may compete mainly with other governments. Defining the market too narrowly hides real competition, while defining it too broadly imports numbers that do not apply.

Market Pricing: Benchmark Jobs and the Market Line

Market pricing connects the internal structure to external data through **benchmark jobs**, the common, stable, well-understood jobs that appear in most surveys. The organization matches its benchmark jobs to survey data, plots the results, and draws a **market pay line** that summarizes what the market pays as job value rises. The unique, non-benchmark jobs are then slotted relative to that line using the internal structure from Chapter 4. In this way the inside and the outside meet: internal alignment orders the jobs, and the market sets the dollars.

Pricing Scarce and Emerging Skills

Benchmark jobs and the market line work well for stable, common roles, but they strain at exactly the place where competition is fiercest: scarce and fast-emerging skills. A salary survey is built around recognizable job titles, yet the skills an organization most needs, in data, cybersecurity, and artificial intelligence, often change faster than survey cycles and do not map neatly onto a title. Pricing those roles means pricing the skill, not just the title.

Doing it well requires moving faster than the annual survey. Organizations increasingly blend traditional survey data with real-time market signals, live job-posting pay ranges, offer-acceptance rates, counteroffer activity, and time-to-fill, to sense where a hot skill is heading before the next survey confirms it. The survey still anchors the structure; the real-time signals tell the manager when a particular skill has broken away from it.

When a skill has genuinely broken away, the answer is often a deliberate premium above the role's market line. The discipline is in the guardrails. A defensible skill premium has a written rationale for when it applies, an approval step so that exceptions do not quietly become the rule, a defined population it covers, and a plan to fold it back into the structure if the skill becomes common. Premiums set this way protect both competitiveness and the internal equity of Chapter 4; premiums granted ad hoc, deal by deal, quietly corrode it.

The opposite danger is overreacting to noise. A skill that spikes one quarter may cool the next, and chasing every fluctuation destabilizes the structure and erodes trust. The judgment market pricing demands here is to separate a durable shift in a skill's value, which deserves a structural response, from short-term volatility, which usually does not. Pricing scarce skills is where external competitiveness is most often won or lost, and where the cost of getting it wrong, in either direction, is highest.

> **CASE · THE RISING PRICE OF THE CIO**
>
> Few roles show the market value of a scarce, fast-moving skill better than the modern chief information officer. Consider Adriana 'Andi' Karaboutis, who began as a programmer at Ford, spent two decades there and at General Motors leading large-scale information-technology and outsourcing efforts, then rose to global chief information

> officer at Dell and chief information officer at Biogen, where she became one of only two women on the executive team and helped lead the company's push into wearable and ingestible 'Medtech' devices.
>
> Her trajectory tracks a market shift. As technology moved from a back-office cost center to a source of new products and customers, the CIO moved into the executive suite, and pay followed. Pricing such a role is exactly the scarce-skill problem this chapter describes: the capability is rare, the market for it is rising fast, and a survey built on last year's titles will understate it.
>
> *The case also carries a fairness dimension. Women remain sharply underrepresented in senior technology roles, so market pricing for these positions intersects with the pay-equity concerns of Chapters 3 and 4. Paying the market for a scarce skill and ensuring that pay is equitable across who holds it are not separate tasks; in California, they are the same task.*

Choosing a Pay Level: Lead, Lag, and Match

With a market line in hand, the organization chooses where to sit, a decision introduced as philosophy in Chapter 2 and made concrete here through percentiles. Paying at the market's fiftieth percentile is a match; paying above it, perhaps at the seventy-fifth, is a lead; paying below it is a lag. Most organizations do not pick one posture for everyone. They lead for scarce or mission-critical roles where losing talent is costly, match for the broad middle, and lag where the work is abundant and cost control matters, provided other rewards make up the difference.

Exhibit 5.1 · Pricing Four Roles Against the Market

The illustration below shows how one employer might price four benchmark roles, matching the broad middle, leading for scarce and critical skills, and holding the line where the labor supply is ample.

Benchmark role	Market 50th percentile	Chosen posture	Why
Administrative Assistant	$52,000	Match	Ample supply; no advantage in paying above market.
Civil Engineer	$108,000	Lead (75th)	Scarce; competes with private firms; lagging invites the sorting problem.
IT Security Analyst	$125,000	Lead (75th)	Critical and fast-moving market; turnover is very costly.

Benchmark role	Market 50th percentile	Chosen posture	Why
Custodian	$44,000	Match / slight lag	Straightforward work; cost control, with strong benefits to compensate.

Note. *Figures are illustrative and for teaching only; real pricing requires current survey data for the organization's defined market.*

Remote Work and Geographic Pay

Market pricing assumes a market, but where is the market for a worker who lives in Fresno, reports to a manager in San Francisco, and never comes to an office? Remote and hybrid work, now permanent for many roles, has unsettled one of compensation's oldest assumptions: that pay should track the local labor market where the office sits. When the office is everywhere and nowhere, an employer must decide which market to price against.

Four models have emerged. Under a national pay model, the organization pays one rate for a role no matter where the employee lives; it is simple and feels equitable, but it overpays in low-cost areas and may still trail the most expensive ones. A geographic-differential model adjusts pay by the cost and market of each employee's location, the approach several large technology firms adopted; it preserves market logic but can feel punitive to a worker who relocates somewhere cheaper and takes a cut for the same work. A hybrid model groups locations into a handful of pay zones or tiers, trading some precision for far less administrative complexity. A role-based model prices the job by its own national or specialized market and largely ignores location, a common choice for scarce, high-demand skills whose talent market is genuinely national.

California sharpens every one of these choices. The gap between a San Francisco or Silicon Valley salary and a Central Valley one is among the widest in the country, so a national rate anchored to coastal pay is expensive, while one anchored to the state average will lose talent in the Bay Area. Pay transparency raises the stakes further: once ranges are posted and visible, employees in different zones can see one another's pay and will expect a clear, defensible reason for any difference. Whatever model an employer chooses, the discipline is the same as the rest of this chapter, namely to define the relevant market deliberately and to be able to explain the choice.

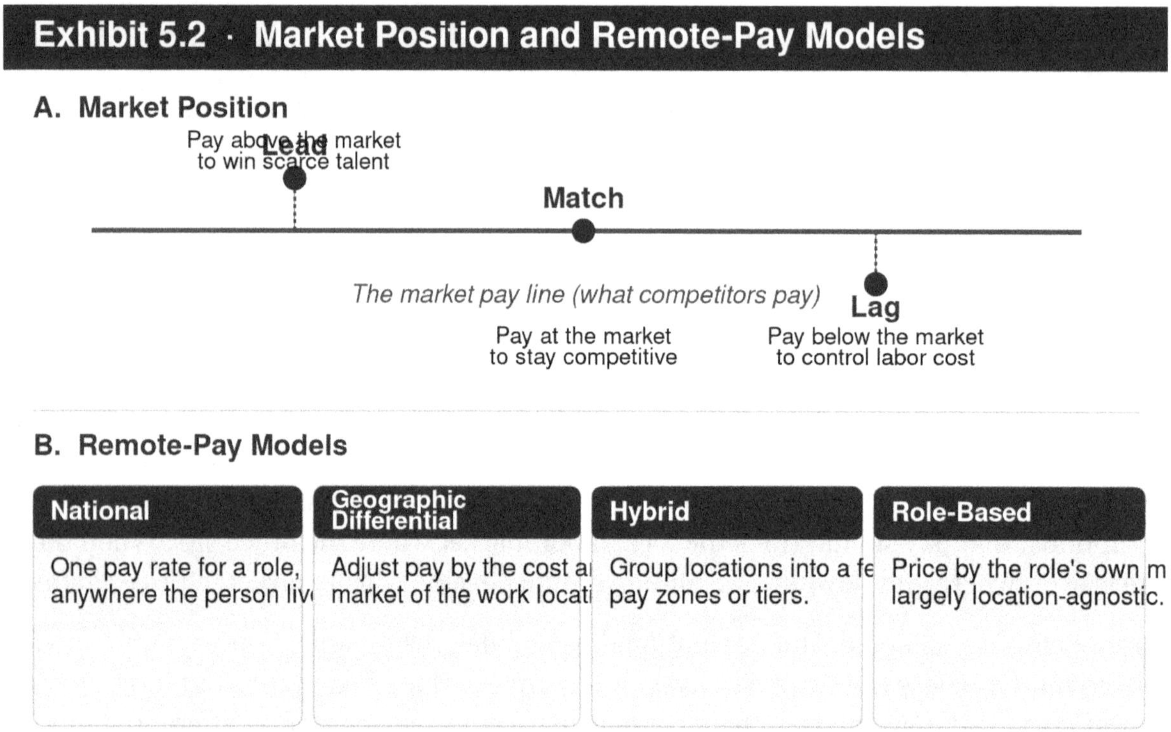

Exhibit 5.2 · Market position (lead, match, lag) and the four remote-pay models.

External Competitiveness versus Internal Equity

Here is the tension that defines the chapter: the market and the internal structure can disagree. When the market for new graduates spikes, an employer may have to pay newcomers nearly as much as veterans, which is fair to the market but feels unfair inside the building, the pay compression discussed in Chapter 4. Comparable-worth findings run the other way, when the market pays a historically female-dominated job less than an internally equal male-dominated one. A compensation manager lives in the gap between these two truths, and deciding when to follow the market and when to honor internal equity is among the hardest and most consequential parts of the job.

Market Pricing in the Public Sector

The public sector prices jobs under special conditions. Salaries are public record, searchable through the State Controller's database, so comparators can read one another's pay precisely. Agencies survey a defined set of peer jurisdictions, and the results are debated openly before councils and boards. Prevailing-wage rules fix pay for many public-works crafts outright. And California's pay-transparency law now places pay ranges in job postings, so the market is increasingly visible to everyone at once: applicants, employees, and competitors alike.

> **CALIFORNIA SPOTLIGHT · TRANSPARENCY MAKES THE MARKET VISIBLE**
>
> For most of history, market pay was semi-secret; you learned what a job paid by applying for it. California has changed that. Under Senate Bill 1162, employers with fifteen or more employees must post pay scales, and any employee may request the scale for their position. Combined with open public-salary databases, a worker can now compare their pay against the market without leaving their desk.
>
> *For employers, the lesson is blunt: set ranges you can defend, because everyone can see them. A range that quietly lags the visible market will just as quietly become a recruiting and retention problem.*

Cost Control and the Limits of the Market

Finally, the market is not a command. An organization cannot, for long, pay a job more than the value that job creates, because labor is a derived demand. Budgets are real, and in the public sector they are set by taxpayers and elected officials. So market pricing always runs back into the value test from Chapter 2: does paying at this level produce a result, in recruiting, retention, or performance, that justifies the cost? The craft is to lead where leading pays for itself and to lag where the savings do no harm.

Conclusion: Three Takeaways

First, a salary survey is only as useful as it is relevant, recent, well-sampled, and matched to real jobs, and it must be aged forward to the date the pay takes effect. Second, price role by role: lead for the scarce and critical, match for the middle, lag only where other rewards compensate. Third, external competitiveness and internal equity will sometimes conflict, and managing that gap, deliberately and transparently, is the heart of the work.

Key Terms

Term	Definition
External competitiveness	The pay relationship between an organization and the employers that compete for the same talent.
Salary survey	An organized collection of pay data for defined jobs in a defined market.
Relevant labor market	The set of employers, defined by occupation, industry, geography, and size, that actually compete for a role.
Benchmark job	A common, stable, well-understood job that appears in most surveys and anchors market pricing.
Market pay line	A line summarizing what the market pays as job value rises.
Market pricing	Matching benchmark jobs to survey data and slotting other jobs relative to the resulting market line.
Percentile	A position in the market distribution; the 50th is the median, used to define match, lead, and lag.
Lead / lag / match	Paying above, below, or at the market, chosen role by role.
Aging (trending) data	Adjusting survey data forward to the date the pay will take effect.
National pay model	Paying one rate for a role regardless of where the employee lives.
Geographic differential	A pay adjustment based on the cost and labor market of an employee's work location.
Derived demand	The principle that labor is paid only because of the value its output creates.
Real-time market data	Current labor signals, such as live job-posting ranges, offer-acceptance rates, and time-to-fill, used alongside surveys to track fast-moving skills.
Skills premium	A deliberate pay add-on above a role's market line for a scarce or emerging skill, governed by written guardrails and an approval process.

Discussion Questions

1. Return to the opening case. Beyond updating the survey, what process should Pine County put in place so its data never falls two years behind again?
2. Choose a role you know. What is its relevant labor market, by occupation, industry, geography, and size, and who are the true comparators?

3. When should an organization lead the market for a role, and when is lagging defensible? Give an example of each.
4. Describe a situation where external competitiveness and internal equity point in opposite directions. How would you resolve it?
5. How does California's pay-scale posting requirement change an employer's market-pricing decisions?
6. Traditional salary surveys lag for fast-moving skills like artificial intelligence and cybersecurity. Describe how you would combine survey data with real-time market signals to price such a role, and what guardrails would keep a skill premium from undermining internal equity.

Applied Case · Pricing Under Pressure

The City of Marina Bay must set pay for three roles at once: a deputy city engineer (private firms are hiring aggressively), an accounting technician (a stable, well-supplied role), and a wastewater operator (a licensed, hard-to-recruit role with few local candidates). The city's survey data is current, but its total salary budget can support a market-leading posture for only one of the three roles.

As the city's compensation analyst, recommend a market posture for each role and defend the trade-offs.

Case questions

1. Define the relevant market for each of the three roles. Where do the comparators differ?
2. Assign a lead, lag, or match posture to each role, and explain which role most deserves the single market-leading budget.
3. For the roles you cannot lead on, which non-cash rewards would help you compete?
4. Run your recommendation through the value test: how would you know, a year later, whether it worked?

References

California State Controller's Office. (2025). *Government compensation in California.* https://publicpay.ca.gov/

California Labor Code section 432.3 and Senate Bill 1162 (2022) (pay scale disclosure).

Ehrenberg, R. G., & Smith, R. S. (2021). Modern labor economics: Theory and public policy (14th ed.). Routledge.

Marshall, A. (1890). Principles of economics. Macmillan.

Milkovich, G. T., Newman, J. M., & Gerhart, B. (2023). *Compensation* (14th ed.). McGraw-Hill Education.

U.S. Bureau of Labor Statistics. (2026). *Occupational employment and wage statistics (OEWS).* https://www.bls.gov/oes/

COMPENSATION: REWARDING AND RETAINING TALENT · CALIFORNIA EDITION
CHAPTER 6

Chapter 6. Base Pay Structure and Administration

Grades, ranges, and keeping a structure healthy over time.

Thomas J. Norman, Ph.D.

Photograph by Thomas J. Norman

> **OPENING CASE · THE RAISE SHE COULD NOT GIVE**
>
> A public-works manager wanted to reward her best engineer, who had carried a major project for two years. When she submitted the raise, human resources sent it back: the engineer was already paid at the maximum of his pay grade, and policy did not allow pay above the range. The manager was frustrated, the engineer felt stuck, and within six months he left for a private firm that simply slotted him into a higher band.
>
> Nothing was wrong with the engineer or the manager. The problem was the structure: a grade whose ceiling no longer matched the work or the market, and a manager who did not understand how the range worked until it blocked her.
>
> *This chapter is about that structure, how pay grades and ranges are built, read, and kept healthy over time.*

Learning Objectives

After studying this chapter, you should be able to do the following:

1. Describe pay grades, ranges, compa-ratios, and range penetration.
2. Explain how base pay is administered over time.
3. Identify the causes and consequences of pay compression.
4. Apply pay-structure tools to hiring and promotion decisions.

From Pricing to Structure

Chapter 5 set pay levels against the market. This chapter turns those levels into the structure employees actually live in: the grades and ranges that determine what a person can be paid today and how far their pay can grow without a promotion. A structure is what keeps thousands of individual pay decisions consistent, defensible, and affordable. Without one, pay becomes a series of one-off negotiations, which is expensive, hard to explain, and, in California, hard to defend.

Grades and Ranges

A **pay grade** groups together jobs of roughly equal value, so they can be paid and managed as a set rather than one at a time. Each grade has a **pay range** with three reference points: a **minimum**, a **midpoint**, and a **maximum**. The midpoint is usually tied to the market, the pay the organization intends for a fully competent performer in that grade. The **range spread**, the distance from minimum to maximum, gives room to pay newcomers less and experienced, high-performing employees more. Spreads tend to be narrower for entry-level work (perhaps 30 to 40 percent) and wider for professional and managerial work (50 percent or more), because skill and performance vary more at higher levels.

Adjacent grades normally overlap, so the top of one grade sits above the bottom of the next. That overlap is healthy: it lets a seasoned employee in a lower grade out-earn a brand-new employee in the grade above, which reflects the value of experience and avoids forcing a promotion just to grant a raise.

Exhibit 6.1 · A Simple Four-Grade Structure

Grade	Minimum	Midpoint	Maximum	Spread
1	$45,000	$54,000	$63,000	40%
2	$54,000	$66,000	$78,000	44%
3	$66,000	$82,500	$99,000	50%
4	$82,000	$105,000	$128,000	56%

Note. *Illustrative figures. Notice that the ranges overlap and that the spread widens in the higher grades.*

Range Spread and Midpoint Progression

Two design choices give a structure its shape. The range spread is the distance from the minimum to the maximum of a grade, expressed as a percentage of the minimum; spreads of thirty to fifty percent are common, with wider spreads at higher grades where careers are longer and performance differences larger. A wide spread gives managers room to reward growth without a promotion; a narrow one keeps pay tightly controlled and consistent. Midpoint progression is the percentage jump between the midpoints of adjacent grades, and it encodes what a promotion is worth: too small, and employees see little reason to take on more; too large, and the structure invites grade inflation. Together, range spread and midpoint progression turn a list of grades into a coherent ladder. Exhibit 6.2 shows the anatomy of a single range.

Exhibit 6.2 · Anatomy of a Pay Range

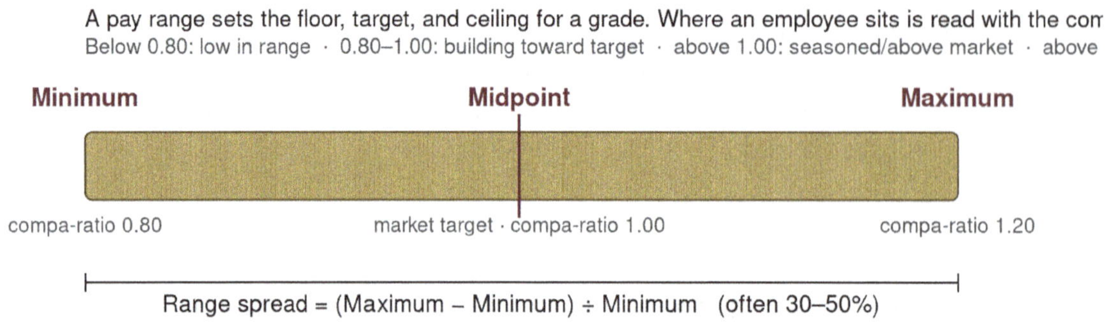

Exhibit 6.2 · The anatomy of a pay range: minimum, midpoint, maximum, range spread, and compa-ratio.

Reading a Pay Range: Compa-Ratio and Range Penetration

Two simple measures tell a manager where an employee sits in a range. The **compa-ratio** is the employee's pay divided by the range midpoint. A compa-ratio of 1.0 means the employee is paid right at the market reference; 0.90 means ten percent below it; 1.10 means ten percent above. **Range penetration** measures how far through the range the employee has moved: pay minus the minimum, divided by the maximum minus the minimum.

Take an employee in Grade 2 (midpoint $66,000, minimum $54,000, maximum $78,000) earning $60,000. Their compa-ratio is 60,000 divided by 66,000, or about 0.91, slightly below market. Their range penetration is 6,000 divided by 24,000, or 25 percent, meaning they are a quarter of the way up the range. Read across a whole department, these numbers reveal patterns: a unit where everyone clusters near the maximum is about to face the very problem from the opening case, while compa-ratios that drift below 0.90 for experienced staff are an early warning of compression.

Broadbanding and Step Systems

Organizations differ in how many grades they use. **Broadbanding** collapses many narrow grades into a few wide bands, giving managers flexibility to move and reward people without constant reclassification; the cost is less control and weaker cost discipline. At the other extreme, public agencies often use **step systems**: many narrow grades, each divided into fixed steps, with advancement governed by written rules. The federal General Schedule is the classic example, with fifteen grades and ten steps each. Step systems are transparent and easy to defend, which is why governments favor them, but they are rigid, and when steps advance more slowly than the market moves, compression follows.

Administering Pay Over Time

A structure is not built once and left alone; it is administered continuously. **Merit increases** move an employee through the range for performance. **Promotions** move an employee into a higher grade, usually with an increase that places them sensibly in the new range. Periodic **structure adjustments** shift the entire set of ranges upward as the market rises, which is the step most often skipped, and the omission is what slowly breaks a structure.

Two special situations recur. A **red-circle rate** is pay above the maximum of the range, often because a job was downgraded or an employee topped out; the usual remedy is to freeze the pay until the range catches up. A **green-circle rate** is pay below the minimum, often a new hire brought in low; the remedy is to bring them to the minimum on a planned schedule. Both signal a structure and a reality that have drifted apart.

> **FROM THE FIELD · THE STRUCTURE NOBODY UPDATED**
>
> In my work reviewing public budgets, the most common structural failure I see is not a badly designed pay structure; it is a reasonable structure that no one adjusted for years while the market moved. Cities and agencies will sometimes leave ranges essentially untouched for a decade, then wonder why they cannot recruit and why their veterans are bunched at the top. Building the structure is the easy part. Maintaining it, range adjustment after range adjustment, is the discipline that actually keeps pay competitive and fair.

Merit Pay and the Merit Matrix

Most base-pay increases run through a merit process that ties a raise to a performance rating. The difficulty is that a flat merit percentage rewards a high performer near the top of the range and one near the bottom equally, even though the second has more room to grow while the first is already paid above market. The merit matrix solves this by setting the increase from two inputs at once: the performance rating and the employee's position in the range, read through the compa-ratio. The largest raises go to strong performers who are still low in the range; increases taper as pay climbs toward the maximum, rewarding contribution while quietly controlling compression and cost. Exhibit 6.3 shows a simplified matrix; real ones are tuned to the merit budget each year.

Exhibit 6.3 · A Simplified Merit Matrix (annual increase %)

Performance rating	Low in range (0.80–0.90)	Below midpoint (0.90–1.00)	Above midpoint (1.00–1.10)	High in range (1.10–1.20)
Outstanding	7%	6%	5%	4%
Exceeds expectations	5%	4%	3%	2%
Meets expectations	3%	2.5%	2%	1.5%
Below expectations	0%	0%	0%	0%

Increases rise with performance and taper as pay climbs the range, rewarding contribution while controlling compression and cost.

Exhibit 6.3 · A merit matrix sets each raise from performance and position in the range.

When the Floor Rises: A California Compression Problem

California adds a distinctive version of this problem at the bottom of the structure. Each time the state minimum wage rises, most recently to $16.90 an hour in 2026, the floor of the lowest grades is pushed up while the grades above them are not, squeezing the differentials that separate entry jobs from the leads and supervisors over them. Left unadjusted, a long-tenured crew lead can end up earning only pennies more than a brand-new hire whose pay was lifted by law, and sectoral floors sharpen the effect: a fast-food worker guaranteed twenty dollars an hour under Assembly Bill 1228 can out-earn the assistant manager one rung up. Administering a structure in California therefore means re-spacing the entire ladder when the floor rises, not merely topping up the bottom rung.

Pay Compression and Inversion, Revisited

Chapter 4 introduced compression and inversion as symptoms of internal misalignment. With the tools of this chapter, we can see the mechanism precisely. Compression happens when range adjustments and step advancement lag a rising external market: new hires must be brought in near the midpoint to compete, while veterans, who advance only slowly, see their compa-ratios fall toward the newcomers'. Inversion is the same process gone further, when a new hire's compa-ratio exceeds a veteran's. The diagnosis lives in the numbers, a cluster of veterans with falling compa-ratios beside new hires near or above midpoint, and the fixes are structural: adjust the ranges to the market, grant targeted equity increases to the affected veterans, or accelerate steps. The Harbor Vista nursing case from Chapter 4 is exactly this story, and so is the Los Angeles Police Department's decision to raise starting pay to compete, which lifted the floor faster than veterans' pay could follow.

Structure in Hiring and Promotion

The everyday power of a structure shows up at two moments. At hiring, the range tells a manager where a candidate can reasonably start: a strong, experienced hire might come in above the minimum but rarely at the maximum, which would leave no room to reward future growth. At promotion, the structure sets a sensible increase and a defensible new position in the higher grade. Used well, the range disciplines these decisions and makes them explainable; ignored, as in the opening case, it surprises managers at the worst possible moment.

CALIFORNIA SPOTLIGHT · THE POSTED RANGE MUST MATCH THE REAL STRUCTURE

California's pay-transparency law (Senate Bill 1162) requires employers with fifteen or more employees to post a pay scale in job listings, and employees may request the scale for their position. That posted range is, in effect, the public face of the internal structure described in this chapter. If the real structure is out of date or inconsistently administered, the posted range will either mislead applicants or expose the gaps to current employees who can now see exactly where they stand.

The practical lesson: in California, a healthy, well-maintained pay structure is no longer just good management. It is a compliance and credibility requirement, because the range is visible to everyone.

ETHICS LENS · WHEN A FAIR RAISE FEELS UNFAIR

Employees judge pay socially, not just arithmetically. A merit increase can be perfectly defensible on the spreadsheet and still feel unjust if it is poorly explained, inconsistently applied, or compared with a newer colleague's higher starting offer. A pay structure is only as good as the communication around it: the same raise lands as a reward or an insult depending on whether the employee understands the range, the rating, and the reasoning behind both. Procedural and interactional fairness, from Chapter 4, are not soft add-ons to a structure; they are what make the numbers believable.

Conclusion: Three Takeaways

First, a pay structure, grades and ranges with a minimum, midpoint, and maximum, turns market levels into consistent, defensible day-to-day decisions. Second, compa-ratio and range penetration let a manager read where people sit and spot trouble early. Third, a structure is only as good as its maintenance: skip the regular range adjustment and compression, inversion, and the raise you cannot give will follow.

Key Terms

Term	Definition
Range spread	The distance from a grade's minimum to its maximum, as a percentage of the minimum (often 30-50%).
Midpoint progression	The percentage increase between the midpoints of adjacent pay grades.
Merit matrix	A grid that sets each merit increase from two inputs: the performance rating and the employee's position in the range (compa-ratio).
Pay grade	A group of jobs of roughly equal value, paid and managed as a set.
Pay range	The minimum, midpoint, and maximum pay for a grade.
Midpoint	The market reference point of a range, the intended pay for a fully competent performer.
Range spread	The distance from a range's minimum to its maximum, usually wider in higher grades.
Compa-ratio	Employee pay divided by the range midpoint; 1.0 means at the market reference.
Range penetration	How far an employee's pay has moved through the range: (pay - minimum) / (maximum - minimum).
Broadbanding	Collapsing many narrow grades into a few wide bands for flexibility.
Step system	Many narrow grades, each with fixed steps and rule-based advancement (e.g., the federal General Schedule).
Structure adjustment	Shifting the whole set of ranges upward as the market rises.
Red-circle rate	Pay above the range maximum, usually frozen until the range catches up.
Green-circle rate	Pay below the range minimum, usually raised on a planned schedule.

Discussion Questions

1. Return to the opening case. What structural options did the manager actually have, and what should the organization have done before she ever submitted the raise?
2. An employee earns $72,000 in a grade with a $66,000 midpoint, a $54,000 minimum, and a $78,000 maximum. Compute the compa-ratio and range penetration, and say what they tell you.

3. When does broadbanding help an organization, and when would a step system serve it better?
4. Why is the periodic structure adjustment the step organizations most often skip, and what happens when they do?
5. How does California's posted-range requirement raise the stakes for keeping a pay structure current?
6. When California raises its minimum wage, the lowest grades' floors rise but the grades above them may not. Explain how this compresses a structure from the bottom, and what a manager should do to keep the differentials intact.

Applied Case · The Structure That Drifted

The City of Alder Grove has not adjusted its pay ranges in eight years. Reviewing the data, you find that most employees with more than six years of service sit within five percent of their range maximums, several recent hires were brought in above the range minimum to compete, and three long-tenured analysts now have lower compa-ratios than analysts hired last year. Turnover among mid-career staff has risen sharply.

The city manager has asked you to diagnose the problem and propose a fix that the council can afford and defend.

Case questions

1. Name precisely what has happened to Alder Grove's structure, using the terms from this chapter.
2. What do the compa-ratio patterns tell you about who is most at risk of leaving?
3. Propose a phased fix (range adjustment, targeted equity increases, or both) and explain the cost and fairness trade-offs.
4. What ongoing administration practice would keep the structure from drifting again?

References

Milkovich, G. T., Newman, J. M., & Gerhart, B. (2023). *Compensation* (14th ed.). McGraw-Hill Education.

U.S. Office of Personnel Management. (2025). *General Schedule (GS) classification and pay*. https://www.opm.gov/policy-data-oversight/pay-leave/pay-systems/general-schedule/

California Labor Code section 432.3 and Senate Bill 1162 (2022) (pay scale disclosure).

COMPENSATION: REWARDING AND RETAINING TALENT · CALIFORNIA EDITION
CHAPTER 7

Chapter 7. Incentive Pay and Performance Management

Paying for performance without paying for the wrong thing.

Thomas J. Norman, Ph.D.

Photograph by Thomas J. Norman

> **OPENING CASE · THE ACCOUNTS THAT WERE NEVER ASKED FOR**
>
> Between 2011 and 2016, employees at Wells Fargo opened roughly 1.5 million deposit accounts and another 565,000 credit-card accounts that customers never requested; later estimates put the total near 3.5 million. They did it to hit aggressive cross-selling sales goals that drove their bonuses.
>
> When it surfaced, regulators including the Consumer Financial Protection Bureau, the Office of the Comptroller of the Currency, and the Los Angeles City Attorney levied a $185 million penalty in 2016. The bank fired about 5,300 employees and later paid $3 billion to resolve federal investigations (NPR, 2016; U.S. Department of Justice, 2020a).
>
> *The incentive worked exactly as designed. It produced more accounts. It simply produced fake ones. That is the paradox at the center of this chapter: incentive pay is the most powerful and the most dangerous tool in compensation, because you get precisely what you pay for.*

Learning Objectives

After studying this chapter, you should be able to do the following:

1. Distinguish among individual, team, and organizational incentives.
2. Explain how incentive plans affect motivation and behavior.
3. Identify common design problems in incentive systems.
4. Evaluate when incentive pay is appropriate and when it is not.

Why Incentives Are Powerful and Dangerous

An incentive is pay made contingent on results: hit the target, earn the reward. Incentives exist because of the problem named in Chapter 2, the agency problem. Owners and managers (principals) cannot watch every action of every employee (agent), so they design pay to make the agent's self-interest line up with the organization's goals (Jensen & Meckling, 1976). Done well, an incentive turns an employee into a partner in the result.

The danger is the mirror image of the power. An incentive rewards the behavior it measures, not the behavior the organization actually wanted. If those two things ever drift apart, the incentive will faithfully produce the measured behavior anyway. Wells Fargo did not want fake accounts; it wanted growth, and it measured accounts opened. The measure and the mission diverged, and the incentive followed the measure. The diagnostic question from earlier chapters returns with force here: what behavior am I actually rewarding, and what behavior am I implicitly punishing?

Types of Incentives

Incentives operate at three levels, and the level matters because of **line of sight**, the clarity with which an employee can see how their own effort affects the payout. **Individual incentives**, such as commissions, piece rates, and individual bonuses, have the strongest line of sight, but they can undermine teamwork. **Team incentives**, such as gainsharing and group goal bonuses, support cooperation but dilute the individual link. **Organizational incentives**, such as profit sharing and employee stock ownership, align everyone with the whole enterprise but have the weakest line of sight, since one person's effort barely moves the company-wide number.

Nucor Steel, from Chapter 2, shows the team approach done well: a transparent productivity bonus that can nearly double take-home pay, with a clear, public formula so every worker can see how harder, better work turns into a bigger check. Strong line of sight, shared gains, and a measure that genuinely tracks the mission, that is the combination to aim for.

Team incentives carry their own behavioral risk: free riding. When a payout is shared but individual effort is hard to see, some members coast on the group's result, the social-loafing problem that grows as teams get larger. Team incentives therefore work best where the work is genuinely interdependent and the group is small enough that members can observe, and gently police, one another's effort. The design task is to keep the line of sight as short as possible even when the reward is collective.

Incentives operate at three levels, and the level shapes how clearly an employee can see the link between effort and reward. Exhibit 7.1 sets the three side by side.

Exhibit 7.1 · Types of Incentive Pay and Line of Sight

Level	Typical forms	Line of sight	Best fit
Individual	Piece rate, commission, individual bonus, merit pay	Strong (direct)	Independent, measurable output
Team / group	Gainsharing, team bonus, shared goals	Moderate	Interdependent work; shared targets
Organizational	Profit sharing, stock / ESOP, org-wide bonus	Weak (diffuse)	Building culture and long-term commitment

As incentives move from individual to organizational, line of sight weakens but cooperation widens.

Exhibit 7.1 · As incentives move from individual to organizational, line of sight weakens but cooperation widens.

How Incentives Shape Behavior

Expectancy theory explains the psychology (Vroom, 1964). People exert effort when they believe three things at once: that effort will produce performance, that performance will produce the reward, and that the reward is something they actually value. Break any link and the incentive goes slack. If targets feel impossible, effort drops; if payouts feel arbitrary, trust drops; if the reward does not matter to the person, nothing happens. And because incentives reward the measured result, measurement becomes the whole game: a poorly chosen metric is not a small flaw but the entire design, because employees will optimize exactly what you count.

Incentives also formalize what management theory calls **reward power**, a leader's capacity to grant outcomes that people value (French & Raven, 1959). A bonus plan turns that power into a standing rule rather than a personal favor, which makes rewards more predictable and more even-handed, but it does not remove the manager from the equation. The leader still sets the goals, judges the performance, and delivers the reward, so a manager's consistency and credibility decide whether an incentive motivates or breeds cynicism. A well-designed plan administered capriciously will still fail.

When Incentives Backfire: An Ethics Arc

Three cases, escalating in harm, show the same mechanism at work. The pharmaceutical company Novartis paid its sales force largely on volume, and a federal investigation found representatives rewarded for prescriptions written regardless of medical need or obtained through kickbacks; the company paid hundreds of millions to settle and then redesigned its plan to reward how sales were achieved. Wells Fargo, from the opening case, rewarded account growth and got millions of fraudulent accounts. Purdue Pharma went furthest of all: its bonus system rewarded representatives for convincing doctors to prescribe higher doses of OxyContin, and a 2013 program intensified marketing to the highest-volume prescribers. The Department of Justice reached a global resolution exceeding $8 billion in 2020, and the company was sentenced in a criminal opioid case in 2026 (U.S. Department of Justice, 2020b; NPR, 2026).

The structural feature is identical in all three: a single, easily measured target (volume, accounts, doses) decoupled from the ethical purpose of the work. The harm escalates from unsafe prescribing to fraud to mass addiction, but the design flaw never changes. Novartis's fix points the way for everyone: make ethics a precondition for the bonus rather than an afterthought, so that how a result is achieved is part of what gets measured and paid.

From the Field: A Quiet Shift in Banking, Minneapolis, Late 1990s

Years before the Wells Fargo scandal, a similar shift was already underway, and my wife and I watched it from inside. In the late 1990s we both worked at US Bank's headquarters in Minneapolis, and we saw the personal-banker role change in front of us. The new hires came from retail sales floors — Foot Locker was a frequent feeder — and they could sell. What they lacked was a background in compliance, which is foundational in lending products. Long-tenured bankers, the ones who had been trained to wait for the right customer rather than chase every prospect, began losing their jobs for being insufficiently aggressive. The institutional vocabulary shifted from prudence to sell now, cross-sell, refer, refer. A few years later, US Bank — along with much of the industry — confronted credit-quality problems that the previous generation of bankers would have priced or declined. The mechanism was the one this chapter has been describing: a single easily measured target, decoupled from the underlying work it was supposed to serve.

What Followed: The Wells Fargo Reform Arc

The Wells Fargo story did not end with the 2016 fine. The bank paid roughly eight billion dollars in penalties and settlements across multiple regulators between 2016 and 2022, including a $1 billion Consumer Financial Protection Bureau penalty and a $500 million Office of the Comptroller of the Currency penalty in 2018 for compliance-risk-management failures (Consumer Financial Protection Bureau, 2018). In the same year, the Federal Reserve imposed an unprecedented asset cap of $1.95 trillion, freezing the bank's growth until it could demonstrate effective governance and risk management. In October 2019 Charlie Scharf, a Jamie Dimon protégé from BNY Mellon, was appointed chief executive with a mandate to rebuild regulator confidence and dismantle the cultural machinery that had produced the scandal. His team built a 3,162-page reform plan with roughly six thousand tasks involving twenty-eight thousand employees, and Scharf made himself the personal point of contact with each major regulator. The Consumer Financial Protection Bureau began terminating consent orders in 2022; twelve of fourteen orders had been resolved by 2024. On June 3, 2025, the Federal Reserve removed the asset cap after seven years (CNBC, 2025; Federal Reserve Board, 2025), and in March 2026 the Fed terminated its remaining 2018 enforcement action. The reform took roughly a decade, cost a documented eight billion dollars in penalties before counting the foregone growth from the asset cap, and required a chief executive willing to confront the culture that had produced the original incentives. The lesson is not that misaligned incentives cannot be fixed. The lesson is what fixing them costs.

What Followed: The Novartis Reform Arc

The Novartis arc tells a different version of the same teaching point: a misaligned incentive can be corrected, but the correction has to reach into the compensation system that produced the harm. The conduct underlying the 2020 settlement spanned approximately a decade, from 2002 to 2011. Federal prosecutors documented over $100 million in payments to doctors through tens of thousands of speaker programs and other events — lavish meals, fishing junkets, golf outings, wine tastings, and sporting events — directed at physicians who prescribed Novartis's cardiovascular and diabetes drugs. The $678 million settlement included $591 million in False Claims Act damages, $38.4 million forfeited under the Anti-Kickback Statute, and $48 million to settle related state Medicaid claims (United States Attorney's Office for the Southern District of New York, 2020).

The "now" arrived in stages. The 2020 Corporate Integrity Agreement with the Department of Health and Human Services Office of Inspector General imposed structural limits on the mechanism that had produced the harm: speaker programs could be conducted only virtually, could not take place in restaurants, could not serve alcohol, and could not pay speakers above industry-norm rates (Office of Inspector General, 2020). The deeper reform, however, was compensatory rather than logistical. Under Vas Narasimhan, who became chief executive in 2018, Novartis recruited Klaus Moosmayer from Siemens as ethics chief and expanded Shannon Klinger's role to Chief Ethics, Risk and Compliance Officer. Sales representatives' variable pay was tied to ethics scores; the chief executive's own compensation package was tied to "building trust" objectives (Liu, 2019). In October 2023, Novartis completed the spin-off of its Sandoz generics business, refocusing the parent company on four therapeutic areas — cardiovascular and metabolic, immunology, neuroscience, and oncology — and concluding a decade-long portfolio transformation (Novartis, 2023).

The teaching point is sharper than the Wells Fargo case in one respect. Novartis did not only police the prohibited behavior; it reached into variable pay and connected ethics to the bonus formula at every level, including the chief executive's. The structural lesson of the original scandal was that the wrong measure produces the wrong behavior. The structural lesson of the reform is that the right measure has to be inserted into the same compensation channel that the wrong measure once occupied.

What Followed: The VA Wait-Time Reform Arc

The Veterans Affairs case completes the comparative set with a different verdict. The original 2014 scandal at the Phoenix VA medical center turned on a single compensation mechanism: performance bonuses were tied to short patient wait times, and staff produced short wait times by manipulating the data — recording official wait averages of 24 days when actual averages were 115 days, and keeping at least 1,700 veterans entirely off the official waiting list (U.S. Department of Veterans Affairs, Office of Inspector General, 2014). The Inspector General documented 17 veteran deaths while waiting for treatment in the Phoenix system, with Acting Secretary Sloan Gibson identifying 18 additional deaths weeks later. Secretary Eric Shinseki resigned on May 30, 2014.

The "now" is the most instructive part of the case. Within months, President Obama signed the Veterans' Access, Choice, and Accountability Act, supplying $16 billion in new funding, $10 billion of which allowed veterans to obtain care outside the VA system. In 2018, the MISSION Act (Public Law 115-182) consolidated and expanded this approach into the Veterans Community Care Program, contracting with more than 300,000 community providers; the number of veterans receiving care from non-VA providers grew from approximately 1.1 million in 2014 to roughly 2.8 million in 2023 (Congressional Budget Office, 2021). Internally, the wait-time bonus metric that had produced the original data manipulation was retired, and the agency shifted to more independent scheduling oversight.

What the reform did not solve was capacity. A 2025 Government Accountability Office review found that the VA had adopted only nine of twenty-seven recommended scheduling improvements and described implementation of the Referral Coordination Initiative as inconsistent (U.S. Government Accountability Office, 2025). The VA Office of Inspector General reported more than 4,400 severe occupational staffing shortages in the first half of fiscal year 2025 — a fifty percent increase over the prior year — with severe shortages for medical officers at 94 percent of facilities and for nurses at 79 percent of facilities (U.S. Department of Veterans Affairs, Office of Inspector General, 2025). The chief operating officer of the Veterans Health Administration acknowledged in April 2026 that current wait-time data show "a mixed picture of improvement and worsening" (Government Executive, 2026).

The teaching point cuts harder than the Wells Fargo or Novartis cases because the VA case is, in part, a story of how compensation reform can succeed at its narrow goal while the larger problem worsens. Removing the perverse incentive ended the data manipulation. It did not produce shorter wait times, because the binding constraint was not the measurement system but the supply of clinicians. For students designing compensation systems, the lesson is that incentive design fixes incentive problems. It does not fix capacity problems, and a reform that addresses only the first while leaving the second unaddressed will look successful in the short term and disappointing in the long term.

What Followed: The Purdue Pharma Reform Arc

The Purdue Pharma arc differs from the others in the most consequential way: the harm it produced is irreversible. The opioid epidemic, into which Purdue's aggressive OxyContin marketing flowed, has been associated with several hundred thousand U.S. overdose deaths over more than two decades. Throughout the late 1990s and 2000s, Purdue's sales force was compensated to visit high-prescribing clinicians, to popularize the now-discredited claim that physicians systematically undertreated chronic pain, and to grow prescription volume. In 2007 the company and three executives pleaded guilty to misbranding OxyContin as less addictive than competing pain medications. In 2020 the company pleaded guilty a second time, to felony charges including conspiracy to defraud the United States and violations of the Anti-Kickback Statute, admitting that between 2007 and 2017 it continued to market opioid products to providers it had reason to believe were diverting prescriptions (U.S. Department of Justice, 2020).

What followed the conduct was an unusual reform mechanism: bankruptcy. The Sackler family, which owned and controlled Purdue, had recognized in advance that opioid litigation would eventually reach them personally and had distributed approximately $11 billion from Purdue to the family — roughly seventy percent of Purdue's revenue in some years — before the company filed for Chapter 11 in 2019. The initial settlement plan included non-consensual third-party releases that would have shielded the Sacklers from individual opioid claims in exchange for partial repayment. In Harrington v. Purdue Pharma L.P. (2024), the U.S. Supreme Court ruled 5–4 that the Bankruptcy Code does not authorize releasing claims against non-debtors without consent (Supreme Court of the United States, 2024). The decision sent the parties back to mediation.

The renegotiated resolution arrived in 2025. A new settlement plan, confirmed by U.S. Bankruptcy Judge Sean Lane on November 14, 2025, requires the Sacklers to contribute up to $7 billion over fifteen years and Purdue itself to contribute approximately $900 million in initial payments, for a total of approximately $7.4 billion (Office of the Attorney General of New York, 2025). Critically, the new structure uses opt-in rather than non-consensual releases: claimants who do not opt in retain the right to sue Sackler family members individually. The Sacklers formally relinquish ownership of the company; Purdue is to be renamed Knoa Pharma under new oversight, with future profits dedicated to opioid-crisis remediation. In April 2026, Purdue received a $5.5 billion criminal sentence as part of the settlement framework (NPR, 2026).

The teaching point completes the comparative set. Wells Fargo's reform rebuilt the institution operationally; Novartis's reform rewired the compensation system; the Veterans Affairs case showed how reform can succeed narrowly while capacity problems worsen. Purdue is the case where the original compensation system produced harm so severe that no internal reform was sufficient — the corporate entity itself had to be dissolved, the controlling family had to be financially confronted through bankruptcy court, and the Supreme Court had to intervene to preserve individual claims against non-debtor family members. The structural lesson is the hardest one. Some incentive systems produce harm at a scale that compensation reform cannot reach; once that point is passed, the legal system has to do the work the compensation system did not.

When the System Undermines the Incentive

Incentives fail quietly, too, without any scandal. Consider a real example from a student in this course. Her team met every performance metric their manager tracked and presented. At payout time, they were told the results had been pooled with another department, one they had never been told about, that had underperformed, and they received nothing. The incentive had worked perfectly: behavior changed, targets were hit. The reward structure then erased the connection between effort and payout. The predictable result is not just one lost bonus but a collapse of trust: in the next cycle, why strain for a target whose reward can be cancelled by a group you cannot see or influence? The lesson is about line of sight and the level at which results are aggregated. An incentive pooled too broadly, or changed after the fact, teaches employees that effort does not pay, which is the opposite of the intended lesson.

The lesson generalizes. Brown (2018) frames it directly: "Clear is kind. Unclear is unkind." Applied to incentive design, this means employees deserve to know in advance which behaviors produce which payouts. When the rules shift in the back room, the system signals that the rules do not matter, and effort migrates from the work to the politics. Clarity in measure, formula, and exception handling is itself a form of fairness.

When Incentives Fit, and When They Do Not

Incentives fit best when individual contribution is measurable, the line of sight is clear, the measure is hard to game, and hitting it genuinely serves the mission. They fit poorly when work is interdependent or qualitative, when the metric is easy to manipulate, or when the real output is hard to count, which is common in the public sector, where much of the value is service quality rather than units produced. The contrast from Chapter 2 holds: a custodial role with straightforward, routine work gains little from a clever incentive, while a parks manager who can grow outside revenue through rentals and youth programs is a natural fit for one. The art is to use incentives where they sharpen behavior and to resist them where they would only invite gaming.

Performance Management and Merit Pay

Most incentive pay runs through performance management. **Merit pay** ties an increase to a performance appraisal and folds it into base salary, so it compounds over a career; a **bonus** is a one-time payout that does not raise the base. Both depend on the quality of the appraisal, and appraisals are imperfect: ratings are subjective, managers vary in severity, and a single number rarely captures a complex job. The research on pay for performance is genuinely mixed, and merit pay has a rocky track record in public education in particular, where outputs are hard to measure and where, as students in this course have noted, poorly designed merit schemes can demoralize as easily as they motivate. None of this means abandoning the link between pay and performance; it means designing the measurement with humility.

It helps to see merit pay as one turn of a larger management cycle rather than a once-a-year verdict. Good performance management runs on a simple loop: set a clear goal, measure progress against it, and adjust, either the behavior or, just as often, the goal itself. The **controlling** function in management is not about catching people doing wrong; it is this Goal-Measure-Adjust cycle, the same logic that lets a pilot hold an altitude or a budget stay on track. Merit pay is simply the moment in that loop where the organization attaches a reward to the measurement. When the loop is healthy, with goals that are current, measures that are trusted, and honest conversation between them, the merit decision feels fair because it confirms what the employee already knew. When the loop is broken, when goals are stale or feedback arrives only at payout, the merit increase becomes a surprise, and a surprise reward teaches very little. The lesson for compensation design is that a merit-pay system is only as good as the management cycle it sits inside.

Incentives in the Public Sector

Public organizations face extra hurdles: budgets are fixed and visible, union agreements may constrain variable pay, and outputs are often qualitative. That does not rule incentives out, but it shifts the toolkit toward gainsharing, recognition, and mission, and toward proactive investment in pay and staffing rather than narrow output bonuses. A police department that invests early and steadily in competitive pay and stable staffing tends to fare better than one that bolts on a quota-style incentive, which is the contrast at the heart of this chapter's applied case. Where an agency can find a clean, gameable-resistant measure tied to real value, such as the parks-revenue example, an incentive can work; where it cannot, recognition and a well-maintained base structure do more good than a fragile bonus.

> **CALIFORNIA SPOTLIGHT · INCENTIVES ARE PAY, TOO**
>
> It is tempting to treat bonuses and incentives as separate from base pay, but California law does not. Incentive pay counts as compensation under the California Equal Pay Act, and it figures into the pay-data reports that larger employers file with the Civil Rights Department. That means disparities in who is eligible for incentives, and in who actually receives them, can create equal-pay exposure just as base-pay gaps do.
>
> *The practical lesson: design incentive eligibility and payout rules to be consistent, documented, and defensible across similar jobs. In a transparent state, an incentive plan that quietly favors one group is not just an ethics problem; it is a legal one.*

Conclusion: Three Takeaways

First, incentive pay is powerful because it gets exactly what it measures, and dangerous for the same reason; choose the measure as if it were the whole strategy, because to your employees it will be. Second, the ethics arc from Novartis to Wells Fargo to Purdue shows one repeating flaw, a single target decoupled from purpose, and one repeating fix, making how results are achieved part of what is rewarded. Third, incentives fit only where contribution is measurable, the line of sight is clear, and the metric resists gaming; everywhere else, a fair base structure and genuine recognition will serve better.

Key Terms

Term	Definition
Incentive pay	Pay made contingent on results or performance.
Agency problem	The difficulty that arises because owners cannot fully observe agents' actions, addressed partly through incentive design.
Line of sight	How clearly an employee can see the link between their own effort and the payout.
Individual incentive	A reward tied to one person's results (commission, piece rate, individual bonus).
Team incentive	A reward tied to group results (gainsharing, group goal bonus).
Organizational incentive	A reward tied to enterprise results (profit sharing, employee stock ownership).
Gainsharing	A team incentive that shares the gains from improved productivity or cost savings.
Merit pay	A performance-based increase folded into base salary.
Bonus	A one-time performance payout that does not raise base pay.
Expectancy theory	Effort depends on believing effort yields performance, performance yields reward, and the reward is valued.
Gaming	Manipulating a metric to earn a reward without producing the intended result.

Discussion Questions

1. Return to the opening case. Identify the single metric Wells Fargo rewarded and explain, using this chapter's ideas, why it produced fraud rather than growth.
2. Trace the common structural feature across Novartis, Wells Fargo, and Purdue. At what scale of harm did regulators intervene in each, and why?
3. Explain the shared-pool failure in terms of line of sight and expectancy theory. How should the plan have been designed?
4. Choose a public-sector role. Is it a good or poor fit for an individual incentive? Justify your answer using the fit criteria in this chapter.
5. How does treating incentive pay as compensation under the California Equal Pay Act change the way you would design a bonus plan?

Applied Case · Two Roads: Wells Fargo and a Police Department

Set two approaches side by side. In the private sector, Wells Fargo bolted aggressive sales incentives onto front-line staff and produced fraud at scale. In the public sector, a city police department facing a staffing crisis chose instead to invest proactively and steadily in competitive base pay, predictable advancement, and stable scheduling, and saw its staffing stabilize without a quota-style bonus. Both were responses to a performance and staffing problem; their incentive logic and their outcomes diverged completely.

You advise a public agency tempted to copy a private-sector sales-incentive plan to boost output.

Case questions

1. What is structurally different about the incentive architecture in the two approaches above?
2. What role does mission clarity play in preventing incentive misfires in a public agency?
3. Design one incentive element the agency could safely adopt, and name the measure, the line of sight, and the safeguard against gaming.
4. Where the agency cannot use a clean incentive, what non-incentive rewards would you recommend instead, and why?

References

Brown, B. (2018). Dare to lead: Brave work. Tough conversations. Whole hearts. Random House.

CNBC. (2025, June 3). Wells Fargo escapes Fed's asset cap after seven years, able to pursue growth. https://www.cnbc.com/2025/06/03/wells-fargo-escapes-feds-asset-cap-after-seven-years-able-to-pursue-growth.html

Congressional Budget Office. (2021). The Veterans Community Care Program: Background and early effects. https://www.cbo.gov/publication/57583

Consumer Financial Protection Bureau. (2018, April 20). Bureau of Consumer Financial Protection announces settlement with Wells Fargo for auto-loan administration and mortgage practices. https://www.consumerfinance.gov/about-us/newsroom/bureau-consumer-financial-protection-announces-settlement-wells-fargo-auto-loan-administration-and-mortgage-practices/

Deci, E. L., & Ryan, R. M. (2000). The "what" and "why" of goal pursuits: Human needs and the self-determination of behavior. Psychological Inquiry, 11(4), 227–268.

Doerr, J. (2018). Measure what matters: How Google, Bono, and the Gates Foundation rock the world with OKRs. Portfolio.

Federal Reserve Board. (2025, June 3). Federal Reserve Board announces termination of the enforcement action it had taken against Wells Fargo & Company in 2018. https://www.federalreserve.gov/newsevents/pressreleases/enforcement20250603a.htm

French, J. R. P., & Raven, B. (1959). The bases of social power. In D. Cartwright (Ed.), *Studies in social power* (pp. 150-167). University of Michigan, Institute for Social Research.

Government Executive. (2026, April). VA has touted appointment wait time reductions, but new data shows a more mixed reality. https://www.govexec.com/management/2026/04/va-appointment-wait-time-reductions-new-data/412883/

Jensen, M. C., & Meckling, W. H. (1976). Theory of the firm: Managerial behavior, agency costs and ownership structure. *Journal of Financial Economics, 3*(4), 305-360.

Liu, A. (2019, January 15). JPM: With new ethics plan, Novartis chief puts his money where his mouth is. Fierce Pharma. https://www.fiercepharma.com/pharma/novartis-hit-by-scandals-over-years-plans-to-publish-ethics-and-compliance-goals-and-link

Milkovich, G. T., Newman, J. M., & Gerhart, B. (2023). *Compensation* (14th ed.). McGraw-Hill Education.

Novartis. (2023, October 4). Novartis executes Sandoz spin-off, completing strategic transformation into a leading, focused innovative medicines company. https://www.novartis.com/news/media-releases/novartis-executes-sandoz-spin-completing-strategic-transformation-leading-focused-innovative-medicines-company

NPR. (2016). *Wells Fargo fined $185 million over creation of fake accounts for bonuses.* https://www.npr.org/sections/thetwo-way/2016/09/08/493130449/

NPR. (2026). *Purdue Pharma sentenced in criminal opioid case while company leaders avoid charges.* https://www.npr.org/2026/04/29/nx-s1-5793938/

Office of Inspector General. (2020). Corporate Integrity Agreement between the Office of Inspector General of the Department of Health and Human Services and Novartis Pharmaceuticals Corporation. U.S. Department of Health and Human Services. https://oig.hhs.gov/fraud/cia/

Office of the Attorney General of New York. (2025, November). Attorney General James secures approval of Purdue bankruptcy plan. https://ag.ny.gov/press-release/2025/attorney-general-james-secures-approval-purdue-bankruptcy-plan

Supreme Court of the United States. (2024). Harrington v. Purdue Pharma L.P., 603 U.S. ___ (No. 23-124). https://www.supremecourt.gov/opinions/23pdf/23-124_8nko.pdf

United States Attorney's Office, Southern District of New York. (2020, July 1). Acting Manhattan U.S. Attorney announces $678 million settlement of fraud lawsuit against Novartis Pharmaceuticals Corporation for operating sham speaker programs. https://www.justice.gov/usao-sdny/pr/acting-manhattan-us-attorney-announces-678-million-settlement-fraud-lawsuit-against

U.S. Department of Justice. (2020a). *Wells Fargo agrees to pay $3 billion to resolve criminal and civil investigations into sales practices.* https://www.justice.gov/archives/opa/pr/wells-fargo-agrees-pay-3-billion

U.S. Department of Justice. (2020b). *Global resolution of criminal and civil investigations with opioid manufacturer Purdue Pharma.* https://www.justice.gov/archives/opa/pr/justice-department-announces-global-resolution-criminal-and-civil-investigations-opioid

U.S. Department of Veterans Affairs, Office of Inspector General. (2014). Review of alleged patient deaths, patient wait times, and scheduling practices at the Phoenix VA Health Care System.

U.S. Department of Veterans Affairs, Office of Inspector General. (2025). Semiannual report to Congress: Issue 93, October 1, 2024–March 31, 2025. https://www.vaoig.gov/semiannual-reports-to-congress

U.S. Government Accountability Office. (2025). Veterans Community Care Program: Improvements needed to help ensure timely access to care (GAO-25-108101). https://www.gao.gov/products/gao-25-108101

Vroom, V. H. (1964). *Work and motivation.* Wiley.

COMPENSATION: REWARDING AND RETAINING TALENT · CALIFORNIA EDITION
CHAPTER 8

Chapter 8. Benefits and Total Rewards

The part of the paycheck that never shows up in the paycheck.

Thomas J. Norman, Ph.D.

Photograph by Thomas J. Norman

> **OPENING CASE · THE PACKAGE, NOT THE WAGE**
>
> Bertha spent more than twenty years as a unionized pharmacy employee. After about five years she had reached the top of her pay scale, around $28 an hour, with solid health coverage and a company retirement match. Then the chain collapsed. A successor grocery pharmacy offered her a similar job at $21 to $22 an hour with no retirement match.
>
> The hourly cut was real, but it was the loss of the match and the benefits that decided her. Rather than accept a worse total package, she changed industries entirely. The wage was only part of what she was actually being paid.
>
> *That is the lesson of this chapter: employees decide on the whole package, the total rewards, and benefits are often the part that tips the decision.*

Learning Objectives

After studying this chapter, you should be able to do the following:

1. Define total rewards and explain its strategic role.
2. Describe how benefits affect attraction and retention.
3. Compare cash and noncash rewards.
4. Analyze how benefits fit a broader compensation strategy.

Defining Total Rewards

Chapter 1 introduced **total rewards** as cash, benefits, and relational returns. This chapter focuses on the second piece, **benefits**, the indirect, largely noncash compensation an employer provides: health coverage, retirement, paid leave, and the protections required by law. Benefits are easy to underestimate because they do not appear in the take-home figure, yet they commonly add roughly thirty percent on top of cash compensation and weigh heavily in employees' decisions to join and stay.

It helps to picture the whole package at once. Exhibit 8.1 shows the total-rewards model: cash compensation, benefits, and relational returns stack together into the single offer an employee actually weighs, and together they drive attraction, retention, motivation, and commitment. The rest of this chapter focuses on the middle layer, benefits, but employees judge the layers as a whole.

From the Field: The Iceberg in Cincinnati, 1992

I joined Procter & Gamble in 1992, right out of Harvard. On one of my first days the company sat new hires down and showed us our compensation as an iceberg. Salary sat above the waterline, slightly above market and deliberately so. Beneath the surface, drawn much larger than the visible portion, sat everything else: a Profit Sharing Trust that vested over time, a generous benefits package, and small unexpected items like organ-transplant insurance that signaled the company's view of an employee's whole life rather than only their current job. The drawing did the rhetorical work of the package: most of what P&G was paying you was below the waterline, and most of it required you to stay.

P&G's profit-sharing tradition was not new. William Cooper Procter introduced it in 1887, one of the earliest profit-sharing programs in American industry. By 1903 the program awarded the dividend in P&G stock; the Profit Sharing Trust in the form I knew it dated to 1944 (Foster & Motley, n.d.). At the end of fiscal 2023 the plan held roughly $21.9 billion in assets across 63,664 participants, with the average participant balance close to $345,000 — and long-tenured employees routinely retired as PST millionaires (Wealthquest Library, n.d.). The folk wisdom in the building when I was there was that anyone who made it seven years would become a millionaire, a claim that compressed the underlying fact that company stock had compounded faster than the average employee could imagine.

Then and now. The architecture I encountered in 1992 has since evolved. P&G's stock-based long-tenure incentives remain, and the PST still anchors a serious retirement story for career employees. But the surrounding philosophy has moved with the broader labor market: more market benchmarking of cash, more recognition that contemporary careers are shorter, and more external hiring for digital and analytic capabilities than the 1990s system ever contemplated. The iceberg is still drawn; it has simply been redrawn with smaller proportions below the waterline and a more deliberate above-the-waterline competitive posture.

Exhibit 8.1 · The Total Rewards Model

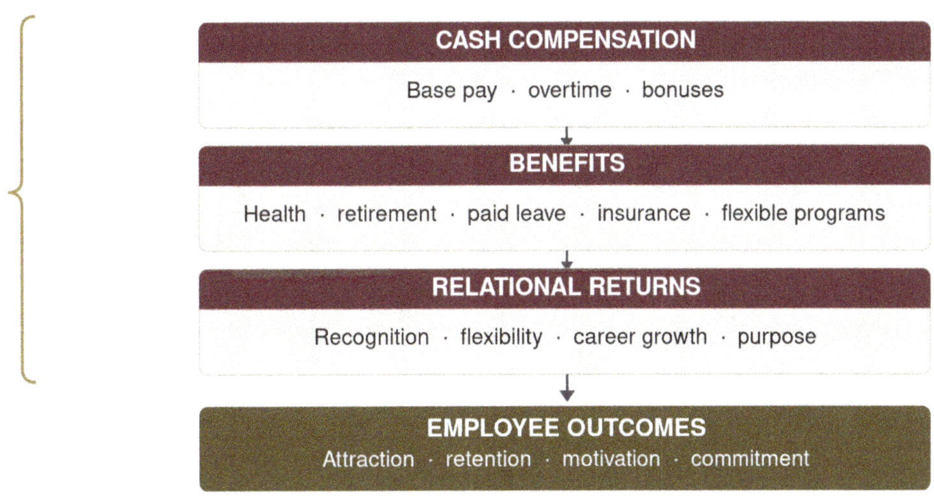

Exhibit 8.1 · Total rewards: cash, benefits, and relational returns combine into one offer.

Why Benefits Matter

Benefits do three things cash alone cannot. They pool risk, spreading the cost of illness, disability, and old age across many people so no single employee is ruined by bad luck. They carry tax advantages, since many benefits are provided with dollars that are not taxed as ordinary income, making a dollar of benefit worth more than a dollar of wage to many employees. And they signal care, telling employees the organization is invested in their security and their families. Because of these features, benefits are a powerful attraction and retention lever, as Bertha's story shows, and they are especially central in the public sector, where rich pensions and stable coverage often offset lower cash pay.

The Major Benefit Categories

Benefits fall into two broad groups. **Legally required benefits** include Social Security and Medicare, unemployment insurance, and workers' compensation, plus, in California, State Disability Insurance and Paid Family Leave. **Voluntary benefits** are those an employer chooses to offer to compete for talent: health, dental, and vision coverage, retirement plans, paid time off beyond the legal minimum, and family-friendly programs. The line between the two keeps moving, because states like California steadily convert what was once voluntary, paid sick leave and retirement access, for example, into a legal floor.

CALIFORNIA SPOTLIGHT · BENEFITS THE STATE REQUIRES

California layers several mandates on top of federal law, and they change often. As of 2026, the key items for a compensation manager are these.

State Disability Insurance and Paid Family Leave. Funded by an employee contribution of 1.3 percent of wages with no wage cap in 2026, SDI provides up to 52 weeks of disability benefits and Paid Family Leave provides up to 8 weeks (California Employment Development Department, 2026).

Paid sick leave. Employees accrue at least one hour for every 30 hours worked, to a usable minimum of 40 hours (five days) per year (California Department of Industrial Relations, 2025).

CalSavers. Effectively every California employer with at least one employee must either offer a qualified retirement plan or register for CalSavers, the state-run retirement program (CalSavers, 2026).

Exhibit 8.2 · California Required Benefits at a Glance (2026)

Program	2026 detail
SDI / PFL contribution	1.3% of wages, no wage cap (employee-paid)
Disability Insurance	Up to 52 weeks of partial wage replacement

Program	2026 detail
Paid Family Leave	Up to 8 weeks of partial wage replacement
Paid sick leave	Accrue 1 hour per 30 worked; at least 40 hours (5 days)/year
Retirement access (CalSavers)	Required for employers with 1+ employee without a qualified plan

Note. *Figures current for 2026; verify with the EDD, DIR, and CalSavers before relying on them.*

Benefit Preferences Across Career Stages

One reason benefits are hard to design is that employees value them differently at different stages of life. An early-career employee often prizes schedule flexibility, student-loan help, remote-work options, and rapid development; a mid-career employee raising a family tends to weigh healthcare quality, dependent coverage, paid family leave, and predictable scheduling; an employee approaching retirement usually values pension security, retirement matching, healthcare continuity, and long-term stability. These are tendencies, not rules, but they explain why a single standardized package can satisfy almost no one fully. Exhibit 8.3 summarizes the pattern.

Exhibit 8.3 · Typical Benefit Priorities Across Career Stages

Early career	Mid-career (family)	Approaching retirement
Schedule flexibility	Healthcare quality	Pension security
Student-loan assistance	Dependent coverage	Retirement matching
Remote-work options	Paid family leave	Healthcare continuity
Rapid development	Predictable scheduling	Long-term stability

Broad tendencies, not rules; they explain why flexible (cafeteria) benefits increasingly outperform a single standard package.

Exhibit 8.3 · Benefit priorities tend to shift across the career and life cycle.

Flexible Benefits and Cafeteria Plans

Because preferences vary so widely, many organizations move away from one fixed package toward a flexible benefits plan, often called a cafeteria plan, that lets employees choose among options within a set employer budget. One employee spends the budget on richer health coverage, dependent care, and extra leave; another puts it toward retirement, tuition assistance, or remote-work support. Flexible plans improve perceived fairness, because employees exercise real control over their own rewards, and they fit a diverse workforce better than any single design. The trade-off is complexity: more administration, more communication, and more employee education, since too many choices can overwhelm people who do not fully grasp the long-term value of what they are selecting.

Cash versus Noncash

Why pay in benefits at all, rather than simply handing employees the cash and letting them buy what they want? Three reasons. Group purchasing makes coverage cheaper than individuals could buy alone; tax treatment makes many benefits worth more than their cash equivalent; and risk pooling protects people from catastrophic costs they would never insure against on their own. The trade-off is that benefits are less visible and less flexible than cash, so a generous benefits package can be undervalued by employees who only watch their take-home pay, which is why communicating the full value of total rewards is itself a management task.

FROM THE FIELD · A REWARD CURRENCY WITHOUT CASH

A startup I advised, Komae, ran an entire reward economy without cash. The venture has since wound down, but the design lesson outlives it. Its app let parents form a private cooperative and swap childcare using points earned by the hour: a parent earned points by hosting other families' children and spent them when she needed care herself. No money changed hands, yet the exchange was real, valued, and motivating.

What makes it a compensation lesson is the structure hiding inside it. The system credited one point per hour for a drop-off but one and a half for hosting at your own home, and it added bonus points for weekends and for watching several children at once. Those were shift differentials and premium pay, expressed in a currency that is not money. The same design logic that sets a night-shift premium or a hardship bonus reappears, untouched, in a care cooperative.

The deeper lesson for total rewards is that reciprocity itself can be a reward. People will invest real effort for recognition, belonging, and the trust that help given will be returned, the relational returns of Chapter 1. A benefits strategy that overlooks this leaves value on the table; one that harnesses it, through care cooperatives, recognition programs, or time banking, can stretch a fixed budget further than cash alone.

Benefits and the Economics of Retention

Benefits shape retention by changing the cost of leaving. Health coverage employees fear losing, retirement plans that reward long service through vesting and matching, and leave and flexibility that are hard to replace all raise the price of walking away. Economists call these switching costs, and the long-term version, a vesting pension or a maturing match, is sometimes called golden handcuffs. Public-sector pensions are the clearest case: a mid-career employee with substantial accrued benefits may stay even when a private employer offers somewhat higher cash. Used well, such benefits reward genuine commitment and stabilize a workforce. Used as the only reason to stay, they backfire, because employees who remain solely because leaving is too costly tend to disengage. Strong benefits work best paired with meaningful work, fair management, and room to grow.

California Spotlight: CalPERS and the Architecture of Public Pensions

The California Public Employees' Retirement System — CalPERS — is the largest public pension fund in the United States and one of the largest pension funds in the world, holding approximately $556 billion in assets under management as of June 30, 2025 (CalPERS, 2025a). It is the canonical example in any California compensation discussion of how a deferred-benefit promise is engineered, funded, and defended over decades.

The defined-benefit promise is straightforward in form and complex in execution. A state or local employee earns a pension benefit each year of service, calculated against their final average compensation and a service-credit formula. The cost of that promise is funded through three channels at once: employer contributions paid out of agency budgets, employee contributions deducted from payroll, and investment returns earned by the fund. For fiscal year 2025–2026, the projected school employer contribution rate is approximately 26.81 percent of payroll (CalPERS, 2025b). The system's preliminary investment return for the year ending June 30, 2025 was 11.6 percent, above its 6.8 percent assumed discount rate, lifting the estimated funded ratio to roughly 79 percent — improved from 71.4 percent in 2023 and 75 percent in 2024 (CalPERS, 2025a). Over the thirty-year period ending June 2025, annualized returns were 7.6 percent.

The "now" of the system is shaped by the Public Employees' Pension Reform Act of 2013, generally called PEPRA. PEPRA established a lower-tier benefit structure for employees hired on or after January 1, 2013, and required them to share half of the "normal cost" of their pension benefits. Approximately 68 percent of CalPERS active members now sit in the PEPRA tier; the share is projected to reach ninety percent within the next decade (CalPERS, n.d.). The structural effect is to bend the long-run cost curve downward without altering the promises made to legacy employees. For compensation designers in the California public sector, the PEPRA threshold matters enormously: the date an employee was hired determines the formula by which their pension benefit will be calculated for the rest of their working life.

Two ongoing debates shape CalPERS's design in 2026 and will continue to do so. The first is climate-investment strategy. CalPERS's Sustainable Investments 2030 strategy aims to roughly double its climate-solution holdings to $100 billion by 2030; current holdings reached approximately $60 billion in mid-2025. Critics have argued that some holdings within the climate-solutions classification include traditional fossil-fuel companies (CalMatters, 2025). CalPERS has resisted full divestment on the argument that influence as a shareholder produces more decarbonization than exit. The second debate is generational equity. The PEPRA tier produces a smaller benefit for new hires than the legacy tier produces for long-tenured employees doing similar work — a familiar two-tier outcome that pension reform necessarily creates. For students designing public-sector total-rewards packages, both debates matter because pensions are simultaneously a labor-market promise, an investment-policy stance, and a political artifact of the era in which they were enacted.

California Spotlight: The San Diego Pension Crisis — A Warning About Return Assumptions

The San Diego pension crisis is the cautionary counterpart to the CalPERS architecture sketched above. In a sequence of decisions in 1996, 2000, and 2002, the San Diego City Employees' Retirement System and the City of San Diego adopted what amounted to a single bargain. SDCERS agreed to grant benefit enhancements to employees. The city, under Mayors Susan Golding (1996) and Dick Murphy (2000, 2002), in turn was permitted to contribute less than the actuarially required amount to fund those enhanced benefits. The implicit assumption underwriting the bargain was that investment returns would exceed the actuarial baseline by enough to close the gap.

Investment returns did not perform on cue. By 2002 a whistleblower's report exposed the underfunding, and a New York Times headline writer would later dub San Diego "Enron by the Sea" (Presidio Sentinel, 2022). The Securities and Exchange Commission investigated municipal-bond disclosures the city had made while the pension shortfall grew. Mayor Dick Murphy resigned in 2005. By 2012 the city had moved Proposition B onto the ballot, replacing pensions with 401(k)-style retirement plans for all new city employees except police officers. The measure passed.

The California Supreme Court ruled in 2018 that Proposition B had been illegally placed on the ballot. State law required the mayor, as chief labor negotiator, to meet and confer with employee unions before placing changes to retirement benefits on the ballot, and Mayor Jerry Sanders had explicitly chosen not to (KPBS Public Media, 2018). A trial court invalidated the measure in 2021, and in 2022 the San Diego city council began the process of restoring pension eligibility for the approximately four thousand employees who had been hired between Proposition B's effective date in 2012 and its invalidation in 2021 (KPBS Public Media, 2022).

The teaching point lands in two places. First, pension promises that depend on optimistic investment-return assumptions are not actually pension promises; they are contingent forecasts that the political layer of the system has dressed up as commitments. When actual returns fall short of assumed returns, the gap is paid by some combination of higher employer contributions, employee contributions, or benefit reductions for new hires, and the political costs of every one of those moves are substantial. Second, even a substantive reform like Proposition B has to be legally defensible, and a measure that bypasses labor-relations process can be struck down years later at far greater cost than the underlying reform would have produced.

Benefits in a Broader Strategy

Benefits should follow the same logic as the rest of the reward system: fit the strategy and the workforce. A young, mobile tech workforce may value flexibility, equity, and learning more than a rich pension, while a public agency competing on stability leans on its defined-benefit pension and dependable coverage as a deliberate differentiator, the lead-where-it-counts idea from Chapter 2 applied to the benefits column. In DART terms, benefits are a major lever of Rewarding and Retaining, and, because they protect families and futures, they carry relational weight out of proportion to their line-item cost.

> **ETHICS & EQUITY LENS · WHO CAN ACTUALLY USE THE BENEFITS?**
> An organization can offer everyone the same benefits and still produce unequal outcomes, because availability and accessibility are not the same thing. Employees on unpredictable schedules may never manage to use tuition reimbursement; lower-paid workers may skip care because the deductible is out of reach; staff in chronically understaffed units may avoid taking leave because it burdens their coworkers. The fair question is therefore not only whether employees have access to a benefit, but whether they can realistically use it. A benefit no one can reach is a line-item cost that buys little loyalty and less goodwill.

Conclusion: Three Takeaways

First, employees decide on the whole package; benefits, though invisible in take-home pay, often tip the decision to join or stay. Second, California keeps converting voluntary benefits into legal floors, so the compliance baseline rises every year. Third, benefits are strategic: matched to the workforce and clearly communicated, they retain people that cash alone would not.

Key Terms

Term	Definition
Flexible (cafeteria) benefit plan	A plan that lets employees choose among benefit options within a fixed employer budget.
Golden handcuffs	Long-term benefits (such as a vesting pension or match) that raise the cost of leaving and encourage employees to stay.
Total-rewards statement	An annual statement showing each employee the full value of cash, benefits, and employer-paid costs.
Total rewards	The full value of employment: cash, benefits, and relational returns.
Benefits	Indirect, largely noncash compensation such as health coverage, retirement, and paid leave.
Legally required benefits	Benefits mandated by law (Social Security, Medicare, unemployment, workers' compensation, and in California SDI and PFL).
Voluntary benefits	Benefits an employer chooses to offer to compete for talent.
State Disability Insurance (SDI)	California program providing partial wage replacement for non-work disabilities, employee-funded.
Paid Family Leave (PFL)	California benefit providing partial wage replacement to care for family or bond with a new child.
CalSavers	California's state-run retirement program for employers without a qualified plan.
Risk pooling	Spreading the cost of uncertain events across many people so no one is ruined by bad luck.

Discussion Questions

1. Return to the opening case. Using the idea of total rewards, explain why the loss of the retirement match mattered more than the hourly cut.
2. Why might an employee undervalue a generous benefits package, and what can an employer do about it?
3. Which California-required benefit do you think most affects an employer's strategy, and why?
4. When does it make sense to compete on benefits rather than cash? Give a public-sector and a private-sector example.
5. How should an employer decide its benefits mix for a workforce that spans early-career and late-career employees?

Applied Case · Designing a Benefits Mix on a Fixed Budget

A California nonprofit with 90 employees can spend no more than a fixed amount per employee on benefits. Its workforce is split between younger program staff who say they want flexibility and student-loan help, and long-tenured administrators who prize health coverage and retirement security. Turnover is rising among the younger group.

As HR director, design a benefits mix within the budget and defend your trade-offs.

Case questions

1. Which benefits are non-negotiable because the law requires them, and what do they cost before any choices are made?
2. How would you split the remaining budget between the two groups, and what do you risk by favoring either?
3. Which noncash or low-cost rewards could address the younger group's concerns without breaking the budget?
4. How would you communicate the total value of the package so employees do not undervalue it?

References

CalMatters. (2025, December). CalPERS' $60 billion investment in 'climate solutions' lacks environmental standards, transparency. https://calmatters.org/commentary/2025/12/calpers-investment-climate-standards-transparency/

CalPERS. (2025a). CalPERS announces preliminary 11.6% return for 2024-25 fiscal year. https://www.calpers.ca.gov/newsroom/calpers-news/2025/calpers-announces-preliminary-116-return-for-2024-25-fiscal-year

CalPERS. (2025b). 2025-26 state employer and employee contribution rates. https://www.calpers.ca.gov/employers/policies-and-procedures/circular-letters/200-025-25

CalPERS. (n.d.). Public agency PEPRA member contributions. https://www.calpers.ca.gov/employers/policies-and-procedures/pension-reform-impacts/public-agency-pepra-member-contributions

CalSavers. (2026). *CalSavers Retirement Savings Program.* https://www.calsavers.com/

California Department of Industrial Relations. (2025). *Paid sick leave.* https://www.dir.ca.gov/dlse/paid_sick_leave.htm

California Employment Development Department. (2026). *Disability Insurance and Paid Family Leave.* https://edd.ca.gov/en/disability/

Encyclopedia.com. (n.d.). William Cooper Procter. https://www.encyclopedia.com/people/social-sciences-and-law/business-leaders/william-cooper-procter

Foster & Motley. (n.d.). Taking the gamble out of retirement: A guide to P&G's retirement plans. https://www.fosterandmotley.com/pg-retirement-plan-services

KPBS Public Media. (2018, August 2). State Supreme Court rules against San Diego pension reform. https://www.kpbs.org/news/2018/aug/02/state-supreme-court-rules-against-san-diego-pensio/

KPBS Public Media. (2022, February 1). San Diego begins to unwind illegal pension reform measure. https://www.kpbs.org/news/local/2022/02/01/san-diego-begins-to-unwind-illegal-pension-reform-measure

Milkovich, G. T., Newman, J. M., & Gerhart, B. (2023). *Compensation* (14th ed.). McGraw-Hill Education.

Presidio Sentinel. (2022). 20 years later, 'Enron by the Sea' still awash in duplicity. https://presidiosentinel.com/local-news/20-years-later-enron-by-the-sea-still-awash-in-duplicity

Wealthquest Library. (n.d.). Managing your P&G Savings Plan and Profit Sharing Trust (PST) accounts. https://www.wqcorp.com/blog/managing-your-p-g-savings-plan-and-profit-sharing-trust-pst-accounts

COMPENSATION: REWARDING AND RETAINING TALENT · CALIFORNIA EDITION

CHAPTER 9

Chapter 9. Recognition, Retention, and Employee Experience

Why people stay, and what pay alone cannot buy.

Thomas J. Norman, Ph.D.

Photograph by Thomas J. Norman

OPENING CASE · THE RAISE WAS NOT THE REASON SHE STAYED

Amy joined a large aerospace and defense firm in an administrative support role. Over several years she grew into culture and engagement work, not because anyone reassigned her, but because she took initiative on visible projects and was noticed for it. Asked what kept her, she points first not to her pay, which was fair, but to recognition and to a clear, transparent path to advance.

Her pay mattered; it had to be competitive or she would have looked elsewhere. But once pay was fair, what retained and motivated her was the experience of being seen, valued, and given a way up.

This chapter is about that experience, the recognition, relational returns, and sense of a future that keep people after the paycheck has done its part.

Learning Objectives

After studying this chapter, you should be able to do the following:

1. Explain how recognition supports retention and motivation.
2. Identify the compensation-related factors that affect turnover.
3. Describe how employee experience shapes reward perceptions.
4. Evaluate retention strategies through a compensation lens.

Recognition and Motivation

Pay gets people in the door and keeps them from leaving over obvious unfairness, but it is a surprisingly weak day-to-day motivator once it is adequate. Decades of research, beginning with Herzberg's distinction between hygiene factors and motivators, suggest that pay mostly prevents dissatisfaction, while recognition, meaningful work, and growth actually drive engagement (Herzberg, 1968). Recognition is cheap, fast, and specific in a way money is not: a manager can acknowledge good work the day it happens, while a raise arrives once a year and is quickly absorbed into normal life. The two are complements, not substitutes; recognition without fair pay feels hollow, and fair pay without recognition feels transactional.

Recognition is the most direct mechanism through which an organization signals that an employee's contribution registers. Froh and Bono (2014) argue that gratitude — the underlying psychology recognition leverages — is a teachable skill rather than a fixed personality trait. Their work on positive youth development demonstrates that gratefulness can be intentionally cultivated through modeling, conversation, and reflective habit, and that the resulting prosocial orientation correlates with engagement, generosity, and contribution to community. The implication for managers is direct: recognition practice is itself a leadership competency, not a soft skill. Doerr (2018) reaches the same point from the operational side. The "R" of his CFR framework — Conversations, Feedback, Recognition — calls for real-time, specific, peer-included acknowledgement that does not wait for a quarterly ceremony. Gallup's Q12 survey captures the same idea in a single empirical question that has predicted engagement and turnover for two decades: "In the last seven days, I have received recognition or praise for doing good work" (Clifton & Harter, 2019).

From the Field: Gratitude as a Workplace Skill — Notes from a CSUDH Colleague

My colleague at California State University, Dominguez Hills, Giacomo Bono, has spent his career studying gratitude. His Youth Gratitude Project, co-led with Jeffrey Froh, has drawn roughly $2.5 million in research funding since 2011 to test whether gratitude can be intentionally cultivated and whether doing so changes downstream outcomes — relationships, school engagement, prosocial behavior. The answer in their work is yes. The translation to workplace recognition is straightforward: gratitude in the manager is the active ingredient that makes recognition feel like recognition rather than a memo. A manager who cannot notice good work cannot consistently signal that good work matters, no matter what the recognition program looks like on paper.

From the Field: How to Motivate Millionaires — Notes from the Tech HR Salons, Late 1990s

I worked at Sun Microsystems in the late 1990s and early 2000s, the years when stock options were minting the largest concentration of new millionaires American industry had ever produced inside a single labor market. The cultural backdrop was the migration of what was then called the HP Way: Hewlett-Packard's famous practice of trusting employees, managing by walking around, sharing profits, and treating job security as a matter of mutual obligation. Sun, Apple, Cisco, and Silicon Graphics had all absorbed parts of that culture. Microsoft, our principal competitor, sat one cultural notch over — leaner, more openly competitive — and was wrestling with the same problem we were.

The problem was new in the same way the wealth was new: how do you motivate employees who are already millionaires? Equity compensation, the lever we had used to build the workforce, had stopped functioning as a marginal motivator. A group of senior tech HR executives began meeting periodically. We met, once, at Microsoft's Redmond campus — which says something about the strange collegiality of the era — and two answers crystallized at that meeting.

The first was the Red Cross answer. People will work hard for a cause that matters more than pay. If the company articulates a mission that organizes meaning around the work, recognition and purpose can do what pay can no longer do. This is the path Sinek (2009) named years later: people do not buy what you do, they buy why you do it. The second answer came from Steve Ballmer, and it borrowed from athletics. The starters on a sports team work harder when they know the bench is watching, and the players on the bench work harder when they believe a starting role is recoverable. Translated into compensation practice, this became stack ranking: a forced distribution that required managers to grade a fixed share of employees as underperformers in every cycle, regardless of absolute performance. Microsoft adopted the system by 1996, with roughly twenty-five percent of employees scored low, forty percent middle, and thirty-five percent high (Eichenwald, 2012). The intellectual provenance was Lazear and Rosen's (1981) tournament theory.

The two answers represented different bets about what wealthy employees would respond to. The mission bet said meaning replaces money. The athletic bet said competition replaces money. The verdict on the second bet arrived in November 2013, when Microsoft formally abandoned stack ranking under chief human-resources officer Lisa Brummel, with current and former employees describing the system as "the most destructive process inside of Microsoft" in widely circulated reporting (Warren, 2013). General Electric and Accenture reached similar conclusions and abandoned similar systems in the same period.

The teaching point for this chapter is that recognition and retention should be designed with a clear-eyed view of what pay can and cannot do. Once compensation has done its job of attracting and basically retaining a workforce, the marginal returns to additional pay decline, and the question becomes which non-monetary system will pick up where pay left off. Mission, recognition, and developmental coaching — the subjects of this chapter — are one answer. Forced competition turned out to be a different answer, and a worse one.

Underneath recognition lies an old but durable distinction: hygiene factors, such as pay and working conditions, prevent dissatisfaction, while motivators, such as recognition and growth, drive engagement. Exhibit 9.1 contrasts the two.

Exhibit 9.1 · Hygiene Factors vs. Motivators

HYGIENE FACTORS Prevent dissatisfaction	MOTIVATORS Drive engagement
• Pay and benefits	• Recognition
• Job security	• Achievement
• Working conditions	• Growth and learning
• Company policy	• Responsibility
• Supervision quality	• Meaningful work

Pay prevents dissatisfaction; recognition and growth drive engagement (after Herzberg).

Exhibit 9.1 · Pay prevents dissatisfaction; recognition and growth drive engagement (after Herzberg).

Why People Leave

Turnover is expensive, often far more than managers assume once recruiting, onboarding, lost productivity, and lost institutional knowledge are counted. Compensation drives turnover in three main ways. The first is external: pay that falls behind the market, the lagging structure of Chapters 5 and 6, makes leaving rational. The second is internal: perceived unfairness relative to coworkers, the compression and equity problems of Chapter 4, drives people out even when their absolute pay is fine. The third is experiential: a lack of recognition, growth, or respect makes employees willing to leave for the same or even slightly less pay, as Bertha's and Amy's stories show from opposite directions. A retention strategy has to address all three, and only the first is purely about the size of the check.

Employee Experience and Reward Perception

Employees do not experience their rewards as a spreadsheet; they experience them as a story about how the organization sees them. The same raise can feel generous or insulting depending on how it is explained, how it compares to peers, and whether the process felt fair, the procedural justice of Chapter 4. This is why pay communication is part of compensation, not an afterthought. A well-designed reward that is poorly communicated will be undervalued, while a modest reward delivered with clarity and genuine recognition can land as far more. In a transparent state, where employees can see ranges and compare, the quality of that communication matters more than ever.

Guidara (2022) gives this idea a vivid frame from the hospitality industry. The Eleven Madison Park principle of one-size-fits-one — recognizing the specific person, not the abstract category — is what transforms a transactional encounter into a memorable one. He pairs this with the 95/5 rule: organizations should be disciplined about ninety-five percent of cost in order to be unreasonable on the five percent that creates the moment people remember. Applied to compensation, this argues for tight cost discipline on base pay and benefits structures, paired with a small reserve for personalized, in-the-moment recognition. Comp committees rarely write the budget this way; the chapter argues they should.

Retention Through a Compensation Lens

Several tools connect compensation to retention directly. Targeted equity adjustments fix the internal unfairness that drives good people out. Stay interviews ask current employees what would keep them before they start looking, which is cheaper than exit interviews that ask after the decision is made. Clear career and pay progression, the visible path Amy valued, lets people see a future without leaving to find one. And recognition programs, formal and informal, keep the relational account in good standing between annual pay actions. None of these replaces competitive pay; each multiplies its effect.

Duckworth (2016) names the trait that pays this off on the employee side. Grit — what she defines as passion and perseverance for very long-term goals — predicts who stays through the difficult periods that any career inevitably contains. Compensation cannot manufacture grit, but it can make staying possible for the people who already carry it: a fair pay trajectory, a credible career path, and recognition that names the long arc of contribution rather than only the most recent quarter.

Mission and Relational Returns in the Public Sector

The public and nonprofit sectors compete for talent on a field where they often cannot win on cash, so relational returns carry extra weight. Mission is the largest of these: people choose teaching, public health, parks, and public safety in part because the work matters to them, and that pull is real compensation. The author's own choice to leave a far larger private offer for a university role, described in Chapter 1, is an ordinary version of a decision public employers rely on every day. The danger is to take mission for granted, treating it as a license to underpay; mission retains people only when pay is fair enough that they are not forced to choose between their values and their families.

Sinek (2009) names the connective tissue. The Golden Circle — Why, How, What — argues that "people don't buy what you do, they buy why you do it" (p. 41). Translated to public-sector employment, this is the engine of mission-based retention: people sign on for the work because the why of public service still moves them, even when the what and the how are bounded by budget and bureaucracy. The compensation system's job is to keep that connection from being eroded by mundane unfairness.

> **CALIFORNIA SPOTLIGHT · TRANSPARENCY AND THE PSYCHOLOGY OF STAYING**
>
> California's pay-transparency rules change the retention conversation. When employees can see the posted range for their own job and for the one above it, fairness is no longer a matter of trust; it is a matter of public record. That cuts both ways. An employer whose pay is fair and whose ranges are well maintained gains credibility, because the numbers back up the story. An employer whose pay has quietly fallen behind loses people faster, because the gap is now visible to the very employees most tempted to leave.
>
> *The lesson: in California, recognition and a fair, transparent structure are not soft extras. They are the retention strategy, because employees can check the math.*

Conclusion: Three Takeaways

First, pay prevents dissatisfaction, but recognition, growth, and meaning drive engagement; budget for both. Second, people leave for three compensation-related reasons, a lagging market, internal unfairness, and a poor experience, and only the first is about the size of the check. Third, in a transparent state, a fair structure plus genuine recognition is the most durable retention tool an employer has.

Key Terms

Term	Definition
Recognition	Timely, specific acknowledgment of good work; a low-cost motivator distinct from pay.
Retention	The organization's ability to keep employees, especially those costly to replace.
Turnover cost	The full cost of losing an employee: recruiting, onboarding, lost productivity, and lost knowledge.
Employee experience	How employees perceive their work, rewards, and treatment over time.
Hygiene factor	A condition (such as pay) whose absence causes dissatisfaction but whose presence does not strongly motivate.
Motivator	A factor (such as recognition, achievement, or growth) that actively drives engagement.
Stay interview	A conversation with a current employee about what would keep them, conducted before they consider leaving.
Relational returns	The non-financial value of work: recognition, status, security, growth, colleagues, and mission.

Discussion Questions

1. Return to the opening case. Once Amy's pay was fair, why did recognition and a transparent path matter more than additional money?
2. Describe the three compensation-related causes of turnover and give an example of each from an organization you know.
3. Why is pay communication part of compensation rather than a separate task?
4. How can a public employer use mission and relational returns without using them as an excuse to underpay?
5. How does California's pay transparency change an employer's retention strategy?

Applied Case · The Quiet Exit

A California county health agency is losing experienced case managers to a neighboring county and to private employers. Exit interviews cite three things in roughly equal measure: pay that has not kept up, a sense that newer hires are paid almost the same, and a feeling that good work goes unnoticed and that there is nowhere to advance. The budget allows only a modest pay increase this year.

As the agency's HR leader, design a retention response that uses the limited pay budget wisely and addresses the non-pay causes as well.

Case questions

1. Map each exit-interview theme to one of the three compensation-related causes of turnover.
2. Given a limited pay budget, where would you spend it for the greatest retention effect, and why?
3. Which non-pay levers (recognition, stay interviews, career paths) would you add, and how would you implement them?
4. How would you communicate the plan so employees experience it as fair?

References

Clifton, J., & Harter, J. (2019). It's the manager: Gallup finds the quality of managers and team leaders is the single biggest factor in your organization's long-term success. Gallup Press.

Doerr, J. (2018). Measure what matters: How Google, Bono, and the Gates Foundation rock the world with OKRs. Portfolio.

Duckworth, A. (2016). Grit: The power of passion and perseverance. Scribner.

Eichenwald, K. (2012, August). Microsoft's lost decade. Vanity Fair. https://www.vanityfair.com/news/business/2012/08/microsoft-lost-mojo-steve-ballmer

Froh, J. J., & Bono, G. (2014). Making grateful kids: The science of building character. Templeton Press.

Guidara, W. (2022). Unreasonable hospitality: The remarkable power of giving people more than they expect. Optimism Press.

Herzberg, F. (1968). One more time: How do you motivate employees? *Harvard Business Review, 46*(1), 53-62.

Lazear, E. P., & Rosen, S. (1981). Rank-order tournaments as optimum labor contracts. Journal of Political Economy, 89(5), 841–864.

Milkovich, G. T., Newman, J. M., & Gerhart, B. (2023). *Compensation* (14th ed.). McGraw-Hill Education.

Sinek, S. (2009). Start with why: How great leaders inspire everyone to take action. Portfolio.

Society for Human Resource Management. (n.d.). *Retention and total rewards.* https://www.shrm.org/

Warren, T. (2013, November 12). Microsoft axes its controversial employee-ranking system. The Verge. https://www.theverge.com/2013/11/12/5094864/microsoft-kills-stack-ranking-internal-structure

Chapter 10. Teaching and Transforming Talent

The development that turns today's hire into tomorrow's performer.

Thomas J. Norman, Ph.D.

Photograph by Thomas J. Norman

> **OPENING CASE · THE RAISE THAT DID NOT WORK**
>
> A manufacturing firm had a long-tenured supervisor whose pay was competitive and whose team was stable, yet whose performance had plateaued. The instinct was to offer another merit increase. It changed nothing.
>
> The problem was not low reward. The supervisor had stopped growing: no cross-training, no new challenges, no development for years. What finally moved performance was not more money but mentoring, redesigned responsibilities, and a path into leadership.
>
> *This is the part of the DART model that compensation cannot buy directly. Teaching and Transforming Talent is the organization's capacity to expand what its people can do, and it is often the missing lever when pay alone falls flat.*

Learning Objectives

After studying this chapter, you should be able to do the following:

1. Define the Teaching and Transforming dimension of the DART model.
2. Explain how development supports performance improvement and role transition.
3. Distinguish selecting for current ability from selecting for future ability.
4. Describe how training, coaching, and development connect to compensation strategy.

The T Dimension

The DART model from Chapter 1 ends with **Teaching and Transforming Talent**, the organization's capacity to increase what its employees can do over time. It is not a training budget; it is a capability. An organization first directs people, assesses and attracts them, and rewards them, and then discovers whether it can grow them. Because performance in the model is multiplicative, a workforce that never develops eventually caps the whole system, no matter how competitive the pay.

Buckingham and Coffman (1999) framed the same insight from the manager's vantage. The world's most effective managers, they wrote, function as catalysts who "speed up the reaction" between an employee's talent and the organization's goals, and between that talent and the customer's needs. The manager's job is not to put in what was left out; it is to draw out what was left in. Buckingham and Clifton (2001) carried the argument further with strengths-based development: a strength is defined as "consistent near-perfect performance in an activity," and the highest leverage in development is found in the area of greatest existing strength, not the area of greatest weakness. The implication for compensation strategy is consequential. Pay systems that reward people for improving in their weakest dimensions tend to produce average performers; pay systems that compound investment in signature strengths tend to produce people who can do work no one else can.

Development and Performance Improvement

The opening case states the chapter's core claim: when ability or opportunity is the constraint, pay cannot fix it, but development can. This is the AMO equation from Chapter 2 in action. If an employee has plateaued because they lack a new skill, training supplies it; if they are blocked by a process or a role that has outgrown them, redesign and stretch assignments restore opportunity. Compensation still matters, it keeps the person from leaving while they grow, but the growth itself comes from teaching, not paying.

Duckworth (2016) traces the mechanism by which ability actually deepens over time. The pattern she describes is deliberate practice — extended, focused effort on tasks just beyond current capability, paired with specific feedback — combined with the long-term passion she names grit. Talent is the starting condition; effort applied to that talent compounds into skill, and skill applied to effort compounds into achievement. Compensation systems should fund the conditions deliberate practice requires: dedicated time, expert feedback, and the patience to defer measurement against the standard while the practitioner is still climbing.

From the Field: A Note from the Harvard Class of 1992

Angela Duckworth and I were classmates in the Harvard Class of 1992. The argument she has developed in the years since — that perseverance and passion for very long-term goals predict outcomes that raw measured ability does not — has reframed how I teach compensation. Pay can sustain a long arc, but it cannot manufacture one. The conditions an organization creates around the pay — the quality of coaching, the dignity of feedback, the visibility of the why — are what determine whether anyone shows up grit-first.

Current Ability versus Future Ability

Chapter 1 noted that Teaching and Transforming is a second-period activity that deepens Assessment and Attraction, because organizations can hire for what a person can do now or for what they could become. A finance team might hire the strongest immediate analyst, or it might hire a candidate with moderate current skill but strong learning agility because the role is expected to change. A health-services employer might pass over the strongest current applicant for one whose adaptability suggests that, after a year of structured development, they will outperform. Each is a defensible choice, but they are different choices, and they imply different investments. An organization that hires for future ability and then fails to develop it has made a bet it refuses to fund.

From the Field: A CEO Has to Start Somewhere — Cincinnati, 1992

When I joined Procter & Gamble's Beauty Care division in 1992, the company had just bought its way into a new industry. P&G had acquired Noxell — and CoverGirl — in 1989 for roughly $1.3 billion, and through the Richardson-Vicks transaction picked up Max Factor and Oil of Olay from Revlon for roughly $1.14 billion in 1991. The Cincinnati culture I joined was famously self-contained. P&G hired entry-level brand assistants out of college, trained them in a deliberate developmental cycle of brand-management apprenticeship, and refused to fill senior roles from outside. The rule applied at every level. The future CEO, whoever that turned out to be, had to come up the same ladder I was standing on.

A.G. Lafley, the executive who would later define the modern P&G, ran exactly that pattern. He joined the brand-management ranks, rose through brand and division leadership, and in 1999 was named president of the global Beauty Care business — the same division I had been hired into. A year later he was named CEO. Bob McDonald, his eventual COO, defended the practice with a startling claim that has since circulated widely in HR research: in companies that hire senior leaders through headhunters, roughly half of those hires fail, while in P&G's promote-from-within system internal promotions almost always succeeded (Kimes, 2009).

Promote-from-within at P&G was not a slogan. It was the architectural choice that justified everything below the waterline in the compensation iceberg. The PST and the deferred package only made sense if the company expected an employee to stay long enough to grow into the work; the developmental investment only made sense if the company expected an employee to stay long enough to become the developer of someone else. Compensation design and talent development were not separate functions; they were one strategy.

Then and now. P&G today is not the P&G of 1992. The internal-tournament edge that defined the up-or-out years softened after the late-1990s leadership crisis and again under Lafley, who pushed the company toward what he called Connect + Develop — open innovation that explicitly acknowledged that the smartest people did not all work at P&G (Lafley & Charan, 2008). The company hires more externally now for digital, analytics, and design capabilities, and the compensation philosophy has tilted toward shorter-cycle, more market-benchmarked structures appropriate to contemporary careers. The architectural insight, though, has aged well: organizations that expect long careers must design compensation that makes long careers possible, and organizations that develop their own leaders cannot also rely on the external market to backfill them. Modern P&G has softened the rule; it has not abandoned the logic.

Plotting current ability against future potential turns these ideas into a practical map for where to invest. Exhibit 10.1 shows the four cases and what each implies for development.

Exhibit 10.1 · Current Ability and Future Potential

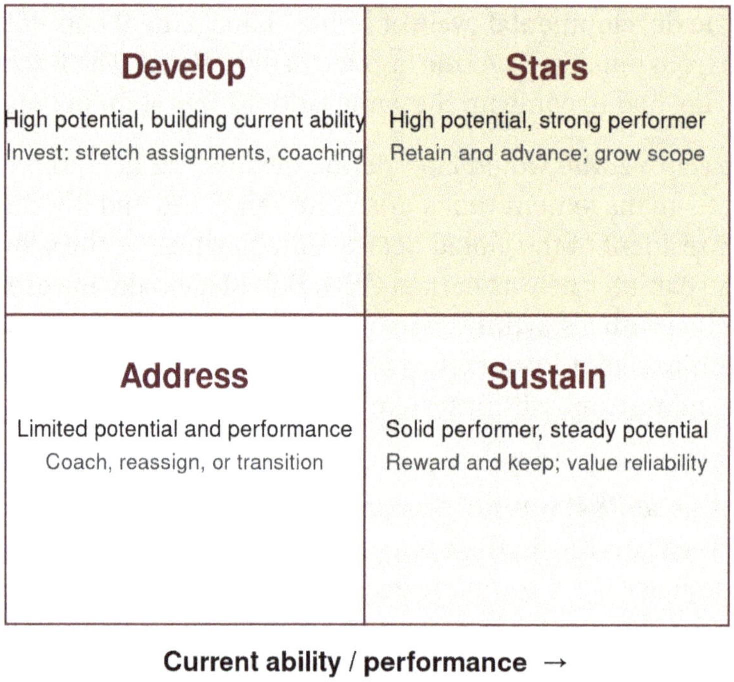

The Teaching-and-Transforming grid: development choices turn on current ability and future potential.

Exhibit 10.1 · The Teaching-and-Transforming grid: development choices turn on current ability and future potential.

The Forms of Development

Development runs along a spectrum from formal to embedded. Onboarding starts a new hire well. Technical training builds specific skills. Coaching and mentoring transfer judgment that no course can teach. Stretch assignments and cross-training grow capability through real work, often at little direct cost. Leadership development prepares people for roles that do not yet exist on the org chart. The most effective organizations blend these rather than relying on a single classroom program, and they treat development as continuous, because, as the lectures in this course note, in a fast-moving economy, and especially in the era of generative AI, jobs can change faster than any annual training plan.

Clifton and Harter (2019) call the underlying transition the shift from boss to coach. Roughly seventy percent of the variance in team engagement, in their dataset, is attributable to the manager — and the modern manager's primary task is ongoing developmental conversation rather than annual judgment. Brown (2012) names the disposition this requires. Daring leadership, in her account, is the willingness to engage vulnerability: to admit what one does not yet know, to ask questions whose answers may be uncomfortable, and to invest in another person's growth without certainty that the investment will pay off. Coaching, in this sense, is not a technique. It is a stance the manager has to choose, and one that becomes easier the more often it is practiced.

Linking Development to Pay and Retention

Development and reward are connected, not separate. **Skill-based pay** rewards employees for acquiring and demonstrating new competencies, paying for what a person can do rather than only the job they hold, the person-based criterion from Chapter 4. Tuition reimbursement and certification stipends, like those some California school districts offer, tie pay directly to development. And development is itself a powerful relational return: the chance to grow is among the strongest reasons capable people stay, as Chapter 9 showed. Treating development as part of the reward package, rather than a cost to be cut in lean years, is one of the clearest signals an employer can send about whether it sees its people as expenses or as investments.

Sinek (2019) places this work inside a longer time horizon. An organization with what he calls a Just Cause — a vision of the future that the work serves — has a coherent reason to develop people whose contribution will outlast any particular project, product, or quarter. Without that horizon, development reads as cost. With it, development reads as the operating system.

> **CALIFORNIA SPOTLIGHT · THE EMPLOYMENT TRAINING PANEL**
>
> California puts public money behind the link between development and competitiveness. The Employment Training Panel (ETP) reimburses employers for approved training that helps them retain skilled workers and stay competitive, funded by a small employer payroll assessment. For a compensation manager, the ETP is a reminder that the state treats workforce development as economic policy.
>
> *The practical lesson: development is not only an internal reward lever. In California, part of it can be co-funded, which lowers the cost of the very investments that keep talent growing and staying (California Employment Training Panel, n.d.).*

Conclusion: Three Takeaways

First, Teaching and Transforming is a capability, not a budget line, and because performance is multiplicative, neglecting it eventually caps the whole system. Second, when ability or opportunity is the constraint, development, not another raise, is the lever that works. Third, tying pay to skill and treating growth as a reward turns development into a retention engine, and in California part of the cost can be co-funded through the Employment Training Panel.

Key Terms

Term	Definition
Teaching and Transforming Talent	The DART dimension capturing an organization's capacity to grow employee capability over time.
Current ability	What an employee can do now, the basis for some selection decisions.
Future ability	What an employee could do after development, the basis for selecting on potential.
Coaching and mentoring	Development that transfers judgment and skill through guided relationships.
Stretch assignment	A challenging task or role used to grow capability through real work.
Skill-based pay	Pay tied to the skills and competencies an employee acquires and demonstrates.
Tuition reimbursement	An employer benefit that funds employee education, linking development to reward.
Employment Training Panel (ETP)	A California program that co-funds approved employer training to retain skilled workers.

Discussion Questions

1. Return to the opening case. Why did another raise fail to move the supervisor's performance, and what did, in terms of the AMO equation?
2. What is the difference between hiring for current ability and hiring for future ability, and what obligation does the second choice create?
3. How does skill-based pay connect development to compensation? What are its risks?
4. Why is development described as a relational return, and how does that affect retention?
5. How might a California employer use the Employment Training Panel as part of its reward strategy?

Applied Case · Hiring for Who They Will Become

A California public-health department must fill several analyst roles. The strongest applicants on current technical skill are also the most expensive and the most likely to leave for private firms within a year. A second group of applicants has moderate current skill but strong learning agility and a stated commitment to public service. The department can fund a structured year-long development program for new hires, but only if it chooses the second group.

As the hiring manager, decide which group to hire and design the development and pay approach that follows from your choice.

Case questions

1. Which group would you hire, and how does the choice reflect current versus future ability?
2. If you hire for future ability, what development must you fund to make the bet pay off?
3. How would you use skill-based pay or stipends to reward growth and encourage staying?
4. How could the Employment Training Panel reduce the cost of your plan?

References

Becker, G. S. (1964). *Human capital: A theoretical and empirical analysis*. University of Chicago Press.

Brown, B. (2012). Daring greatly: How the courage to be vulnerable transforms the way we live, love, parent, and lead. Gotham Books.

Buckingham, M., & Clifton, D. O. (2001). Now, discover your strengths. Free Press.

Buckingham, M., & Coffman, C. (1999). First, break all the rules: What the world's greatest managers do differently. Simon & Schuster.

California Employment Training Panel. (n.d.). *About ETP*. https://etp.ca.gov/

Clifton, J., & Harter, J. (2019). It's the manager: Gallup finds the quality of managers and team leaders is the single biggest factor in your organization's long-term success. Gallup Press.

Duckworth, A. (2016). Grit: The power of passion and perseverance. Scribner.

Kimes, M. (2009, May 20). P&G promotes from within. Fortune. https://archive.fortune.com/2009/05/20/news/companies/kimes_lafley.fortune/index.htm

Lafley, A. G., & Charan, R. (2008). The game-changer: How you can drive revenue and profit growth with innovation. Crown Business.

Milkovich, G. T., Newman, J. M., & Gerhart, B. (2023). *Compensation* (14th ed.). McGraw-Hill Education.

Sinek, S. (2019). The infinite game. Portfolio.

Chapter 11. Measuring Reward System Effectiveness

Knowing whether the reward system is actually working.

Thomas J. Norman, Ph.D.

Photograph by Thomas J. Norman

> **OPENING CASE · A BIG RAISE AND NO WAY TO KNOW**
>
> A California city, worried about turnover, won approval for an across-the-board pay increase. It was a real investment, the largest in years. Twelve months later, the city council asked a simple question: did it work? Had turnover fallen? Were the hardest jobs easier to fill? Was pay now fairer? No one could answer, because no one had set a baseline or chosen a single metric to track.
>
> Compensation is usually an organization's largest expense, yet it is among the least measured. The city had spent the money on faith.
>
> *This chapter is about replacing faith with evidence: the metrics that tell a manager whether a reward system is fair, competitive, and worth its cost.*

Learning Objectives

After studying this chapter, you should be able to do the following:

1. Identify the metrics used to evaluate compensation effectiveness.
2. Assess fairness, competitiveness, retention, and performance impact.
3. Use data to evaluate whether a reward system is working.
4. Recommend improvements to a weak compensation system.

Why Measure

Every earlier chapter made a promise: a fair structure retains people, a competitive posture attracts them, a good incentive changes behavior. Measurement is how an organization checks whether those promises came true. Without it, compensation decisions rest on anecdote and instinct, and, as the opening case shows, leaders cannot defend the spending or improve it. The discipline is the value test from Chapter 2, made routine: for every reward dollar, can we show a result that justifies the cost?

Doerr (2018) gives measurement its purest formulation. The OKR — Objective and Key Results — is at heart a definition of success specified in advance. An Objective says what success looks like in plain language; Key Results say how anyone will know. The discipline the framework imposes is intolerance of vague intent: if a goal cannot be reduced to a measurable Key Result, it is not yet a goal, only a wish. The four "superpowers" Doerr names — Focus, Align, Track, Stretch — describe what well-built measures do for the organization rather than to it. The danger is the mirror image. Sinek (2019) reminds us that some of the most important work organizations do is played on an infinite field — public safety, education, public health — where there is no terminal scoreboard. A finite-game metric applied to an infinite-game mission tends to distort the mission. Both moves are necessary at once: measure what can be measured, and stay honest about what cannot.

The Core Metrics

A handful of measures, most introduced in earlier chapters, form the toolkit. Compa-ratio and range-penetration distributions show whether people sit sensibly in their ranges or have drifted high or low. Turnover and retention rates, especially among high performers and in critical roles, show whether the system keeps the people it must. Time-to-fill and offer-acceptance rates show whether pay is competitive enough to attract talent. A pay-equity or pay-gap analysis shows whether similar work is paid similarly. And cost measures, compensation as a share of the budget and the cost of turnover, show whether the system is affordable. The art is choosing the few metrics that match the organization's goals rather than drowning in all of them.

Engagement deserves a measurement note of its own. Gallup's Q12, validated across roughly forty-five million respondents, links employee perceptions to revenue, turnover, and safety outcomes (Clifton & Harter, 2019). For a compensation manager, the value of Q12 is not the headline engagement score but its diagnostic power: Item 4 ("In the last seven days, I have received recognition or praise for doing good work") and Item 10 ("I have a best friend at work") move when recognition and culture improve, while items linked to clarity, equipment, and growth move when structure and development improve. The instrument lets you tell which lever produced the gain.

Exhibit 11.1 · A Reward-System Scorecard

Metric	What it tells you	A healthy signal
Compa-ratio distribution	Where employees sit relative to market	Most near 1.0; few stuck at min or max
Regretted-turnover rate	Whether you keep the people you meant to keep	Low and stable, especially in key roles
Time-to-fill / acceptance	Whether pay attracts talent	Short fills; most offers accepted
Pay-gap analysis	Whether similar work is paid similarly	No unexplained gaps by group
Cost of turnover	The price of losing people	Falling as retention improves

Track a handful of metrics over time; healthy signals beat single snapshots.

Exhibit 11.1 · A reward-system scorecard: a few metrics, each with a healthy signal.

Note. *A scorecard works only against a baseline; measure before a change so you can detect its effect after.*

Assessing Fairness, Competitiveness, Retention, and Performance

Read the metrics in four lenses. For fairness, a pay-equity audit and compression checks (compa-ratios of veterans versus new hires) reveal internal problems before they become lawsuits or resignations. For competitiveness, market ratios, quit rates, and offer-acceptance rates reveal whether the organization is winning or losing in the labor market. For retention, regretted-turnover and high-performer-retention rates separate healthy churn from damaging loss. For performance impact, the hardest lens, the organization tries to connect reward changes to outcomes such as productivity, service quality, or fewer compliance failures, accepting that the link is rarely clean and never the only cause.

A Metric for Each Element of DART

Because this book is organized around the DART model, it helps to close the loop by attaching a measure to each of its elements. The four lenses above map naturally onto DART: a reward system can be judged by how well it directs, attracts, rewards, and develops talent. The table below pairs each element with the question it answers and one practical metric a manager can actually track.

Exhibit 11.2 · A Metric for Each Element of DART

DART element	The question it answers	An example metric
Direction & Deployment	Are people in roles aligned with the mission?	Share of staff whose goals map to strategic priorities; internal-fill rate for key roles
Assessment & Attraction	Can we attract and select the talent we need?	Offer-acceptance rate, time-to-fill, and quality-of-hire
Rewarding & Retaining	Do rewards keep and motivate our best people?	Regretted-turnover rate and compa-ratio distribution
Teaching & Transforming	Are we growing talent over time?	Promotion-from-within rate and skill or certification growth

Note. *No single number captures an element; pick the one or two that fit the organization's strategy and track them against a baseline.*

Using Data to Evaluate, and to Decide

Metrics earn their keep only when they drive decisions. A simple compensation dashboard, reviewed on a regular cadence, turns scattered numbers into a story: ranges drifting, a unit's turnover climbing, a gap widening. The point is not to admire the data but to act on it, to trigger a range adjustment, an equity correction, or a market re-survey before a problem becomes a crisis. And the baseline matters: the opening-case city failed not because it lacked data afterward but because it never measured before, so it had nothing to compare against.

Brown's (2015) Rising Strong gives the reassessment step its own language. After a reward-system change does not perform as intended, the temptation is to bury the report or to blame the people. The more useful sequence is what she calls the reckoning, the rumble, and the revolution: name what is actually felt about the result, interrogate the story being told about why it happened, and only then design the next move. A reward-system reassessment that skips the rumble — the messy step of testing the assumptions that produced the failure — tends to ratify the original design rather than improve it.

From Annual Review to Continuous Performance Management: OKRs and CFRs

Most large organizations now treat the annual performance review as a problem to be solved rather than a process to be defended. Doerr (2018) traces a complementary system that originated at Intel under Andy Grove and spread to Google: Objectives and Key Results, or OKRs. An Objective states what the team wants to accomplish — qualitative, ambitious, and time-bounded. Each Objective carries three to five Key Results, the measurable indicators that signal success. Doerr identifies four "superpowers" the framework provides: Focus and Commit to Priorities, Align and Connect for Teamwork, Track for Accountability, and Stretch for Amazing Results.

OKRs alone are a goal-setting framework, not a performance-management system. The pairing Doerr emphasizes is CFRs: Conversations, Feedback, and Recognition. Conversations are ongoing one-on-ones between manager and contributor about progress and obstacles. Feedback is mutual, specific, and timely — closing the gap between intention and action. Recognition is real-time acknowledgement of contribution, often peer-to-peer. Doerr describes CFRs as giving OKRs "their human voice," and the cadence is meant to replace the annual review, not augment it.

The implications for incentive design are sharper than they first appear. Doerr argues that OKRs should not be tightly bonus-linked, because tight linkage encourages employees to sandbag their objectives — to set goals they know they can hit rather than goals that stretch the organization. Many practitioners disagree, contending that disciplined guardrails make pay-OKR linkage workable. Both views deserve attention. What is harder to dispute is the underlying claim that effective performance management is continuous, conversational, and recognition-rich, regardless of whether the bonus formula touches the OKR scoreboard.

Brown's (2018) framework reinforces the conversational mandate. Daring leadership, in her account, is a set of skills that are teachable, observable, and measurable; the discipline most relevant to compensation is the willingness to deliver clear feedback in real time rather than file it under a future review.

Reward Governance and Reassessment

Measurement closes the loop of the four-step strategy process from Chapter 2: assess, choose, implement, and reassess. Reassessment is governance, a scheduled, accountable review of whether the reward system still fits the strategy, the market, and the law. Private firms in fast markets reassess often; public agencies, the lectures in this course note, too often leave structures untouched for years and then wonder why they cannot compete.

Building a regular review, annually for metrics and at least every few years for the structure itself, is what keeps a reward system from quietly decaying.

> **CALIFORNIA SPOTLIGHT · THE PAY-DATA REPORT AS A MIRROR**
> California hands larger employers a measurement tool whether they want it or not. The annual pay-data report filed with the Civil Rights Department compiles pay by job category, sex, race, and ethnicity across pay bands. Compiling it forces an organization to look at its own distributions, and, as the Chapter 3 case showed, that look often surfaces gaps no one intended.
>
> *The lesson: treat the pay-data report not as a compliance chore but as a free annual mirror. An organization that reads it honestly learns where its reward system is failing the fairness test before a regulator or an employee points it out.*

Conclusion: Three Takeaways

First, compensation is usually the largest expense and the least measured; fix that by choosing a few metrics tied to your goals and setting a baseline before you act. Second, read the numbers through four lenses, fairness, competitiveness, retention, and performance, and use a dashboard to drive decisions rather than just describe the past. Third, reassessment is governance: schedule it, or the system will decay between crises.

Key Terms

Term	Definition
Compa-ratio distribution	The spread of employees' compa-ratios, showing whether pay sits sensibly in ranges.
Regretted turnover	Departures of employees the organization wanted to keep.
Time-to-fill	How long a vacancy stays open, a signal of competitiveness.
Offer-acceptance rate	The share of job offers candidates accept, a signal of market position.
Pay-equity audit	A structured analysis of whether similar work is paid similarly across groups.
Cost of turnover	The full cost of replacing an employee, used to value retention.
Compensation dashboard	A regular summary of key reward metrics used to drive decisions.
Reassessment	The scheduled review that closes the strategy loop and keeps the system current.

Discussion Questions

1. Return to the opening case. What single baseline measurement, taken before the raise, would have let the city answer the council's question?
2. Choose three metrics from the scorecard for an organization you know and explain why those three fit its goals.
3. Why is performance impact the hardest of the four lenses to measure, and how would you approach it anyway?
4. How can a compensation dashboard change behavior rather than just describe the past?
5. How can a California employer use its required pay-data report as a measurement and improvement tool?

Applied Case · Building the Scorecard

A California special district has never formally measured its compensation system. Turnover feels high, managers complain they cannot fill technical roles, and a recent grievance alleged unfair pay between two similar units. The board has asked you to build a simple measurement framework that the district can sustain with limited staff.

As the district's analyst, design a compensation scorecard and a review cadence.

Case questions

1. Which five metrics would you put on the scorecard, and what baseline would you capture first?
2. How would each metric map to fairness, competitiveness, retention, or performance?
3. How often would you review the metrics and the structure itself, and who would be accountable?
4. How would you use the state pay-data report to support the fairness portion of the scorecard?

References

Brown, B. (2015). Rising strong: How the ability to reset transforms the way we live, love, parent, and lead. Spiegel & Grau.

California Civil Rights Department. (2026). *Pay data reporting*. https://calcivilrights.ca.gov/paydatareporting/

Clifton, J., & Harter, J. (2019). It's the manager: Gallup finds the quality of managers and team leaders is the single biggest factor in your organization's long-term success. Gallup Press.

Doerr, J. (2018). Measure what matters: How Google, Bono, and the Gates Foundation rock the world with OKRs. Portfolio.

Milkovich, G. T., Newman, J. M., & Gerhart, B. (2023). *Compensation* (14th ed.). McGraw-Hill Education.

Sinek, S. (2019). The infinite game. Portfolio.

WorldatWork. (n.d.). *Compensation metrics and analytics*. https://worldatwork.org/

COMPENSATION: REWARDING AND RETAINING TALENT · CALIFORNIA EDITION
CHAPTER 12

Chapter 12. Designing and Defending a Compensation System: California Applications

Putting it all together into a coherent, defensible reward system.

Thomas J. Norman, Ph.D.

Photograph by Thomas J. Norman

OPENING CASE · THE CYCLE THE CLASS COULD NOT STOP

Across this course, students returned again and again to one organization: a large California school district trapped in a self-reinforcing cycle. Union step-and-lane schedules rewarded time over performance. Enrollment-based funding tied the budget to attendance, which fell as quality slipped. The region's cost of living made even mission-driven employees feel underpaid. Internal equity and external competitiveness pulled in opposite directions. And a superintendent-pay controversy made every decision a public agency problem in real time.

No single fix worked, because the problem was systemic. Pay alone could not solve it; neither could a new incentive, a market adjustment, or a recognition program on its own.

That is the challenge of this final chapter: to stop seeing compensation as a series of separate decisions and to design a whole system, coherent enough to break a cycle and defensible enough to survive California's scrutiny.

Learning Objectives

After studying this chapter, you should be able to do the following:

1. Integrate the major concepts of the book into a coherent reward system.
2. Build a compensation approach aligned with the DART model and organizational strategy.
3. Balance cost, fairness, compliance, and motivation in system design.
4. Defend compensation choices using theory, evidence, and California law.

From Parts to a System

Every chapter in this book built one component. This chapter assembles them. The DART model from Chapter 1 supplies the frame, reminding us that rewards work only inside a larger talent system of direction, attraction, reward, and development. The pay model supplies the toolkit: objectives, policy choices, and techniques. A compensation system is what results when those components are made to fit one another and the organization, so that the structure, the market posture, the incentives, the benefits, and the development all point the same way. Incoherence, not any single bad choice, is what most often breaks a reward system, which is why the LAUSD cycle resisted every isolated fix.

A Design Sequence

The chapters of this book also describe an order of operations. One does not price jobs before valuing them, or build a structure before knowing the market. The sequence below maps each design step to the chapter that develops it and the question it answers.

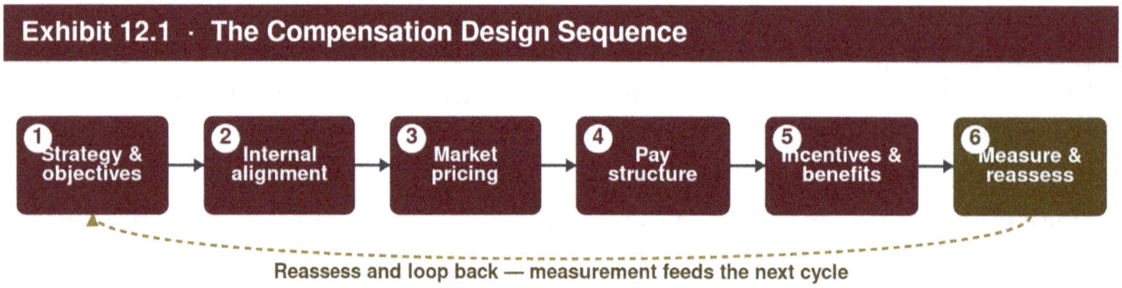

A coherent system is built in sequence and looped back through measurement.

Exhibit 12.1 · A coherent system is built in sequence and looped back through measurement.

Design step	Chapters	Key question
Set strategy and philosophy	1-2	What are we trying to achieve, and how do we compete?
Map the legal environment	3	What does California require of us?
Value the work internally	4	What is each job worth to us?
Price against the market	5	What does the relevant market pay?
Build and administer structure	6	What grades and ranges, kept current?
Design incentives	7	Where does pay-for-performance fit, safely?
Design benefits and total rewards	8	What does the whole package look like?
Retain through experience	9	Why will people stay?
Develop talent	10	How do we grow capability over time?
Measure and reassess	11	Is it working, and is it fair?

Note. *The steps are iterative, not strictly linear; measurement (step 10) feeds back into strategy (step 1).*

Balancing the Four Goals

The pay model's four objectives, efficiency, fairness, ethics, and compliance, rarely align perfectly, and design is largely the work of balancing them. Leading the market for a critical role serves efficiency but strains the budget; compressing differentials serves a sense of fairness but may dull individual incentive; a powerful incentive serves efficiency but, as

Chapter 7 showed, can threaten ethics; and California's compliance demands can constrain all of the above. There is no formula that resolves these tensions; there is only judgment, made transparent. The strongest designs do not pretend the trade-offs away. They name them, choose deliberately, and explain the choice.

Defending Decisions

In a transparent state, designing well is not enough; the design must be defensible to employees, unions, elected officials, regulators, and sometimes a court. Three habits from this book make a decision defensible. First, the 'so what?' test from Chapter 2: be able to say what objective a practice serves and why. Second, the three tests, alignment, differentiation, and value: show that the design fits the mission, distinguishes the organization where it must, and produces a result worth its cost. Third, evidence: document the job analysis, the survey data, the structure, and the metrics, so that a pay difference rests on the real content of the work and not on assumptions about who does it. Theory explains, evidence proves, and California law sets the floor; a defensible decision uses all three.

The design must also be reformable. Sinek (2019) names what he calls existential flexibility — the willingness to make a major change to a chosen strategy when the conditions that made the original choice sensible have shifted. Compensation systems decay slowly enough that the moment to redesign almost always passes unnoticed; existential flexibility is the discipline of recognizing the moment anyway. When a redesign does become necessary, Brown's (2015) Rising Strong gives the post-mortem its sequence. Reckon with what is actually felt about the system that failed. Rumble with the stories being told about why it failed. Only then design the revolution. Reward-system reassessments that skip the rumble — the messy step of testing the assumptions that produced the failure — tend to ratify the original design rather than improve it. The P&G evolution traced through Chapters 8 and 10 is one extended case of existential flexibility done well: an admired classical system, redesigned in stages as the conditions that justified it gave way, with enough of the original logic preserved to remain coherent.

California Applications

Return to the cases that ran through the course. The LAUSD vicious circle yields not to a raise but to a system: a strategy that names the mission, a structure adjusted to the market, targeted equity fixes for compression, and development and recognition that pay alone cannot supply. The FAA's virtuous circle shows the same systemic logic succeeding, a multi-lever workforce plan that combined starting pay, retention bonuses, hard-to-staff incentives, and a faster pipeline. The Wells Fargo and Phoenix contrast warns that an incentive bolted onto a weak system produces harm, while patient investment in a sound one produces stability. Each case, read through the whole book, teaches the same lesson: coherent systems beat clever fragments.

> **CALIFORNIA SPOTLIGHT · DESIGNED TO BE SEEN**
>
> Everything in this book lands, in California, on a single fact: the system will be seen. Pay scales appear in job postings, public salaries are searchable, larger employers file pay-data reports, and the Equal Pay Act asks employers to justify differences in substantially similar work. A compensation system designed in California is, in effect, designed for an audience.
>
> *That is not a burden so much as a discipline. A reward system built to be defended in the open, documented, equitable, and explainable, is simply a better system. Transparency does not make good compensation harder; it makes bad compensation impossible to hide.*

Conclusion: The Argument of the Book

This book began with a simple claim: organizations perform better when they reward talent well, but rewards work only inside a larger system. Twelve chapters later, the claim has a shape. Use the DART model to keep reward connected to direction, attraction, and development. Use the pay model to make the choices. Sequence the work so each step rests on the last. Balance efficiency, fairness, ethics, and compliance with named, deliberate judgment. And, especially in California, design every piece to be seen and defended. Do that, and the question every employee asks, am I being paid what I am worth, becomes one the organization can answer with confidence.

Key Terms

Term	Definition
Compensation system	The integrated set of strategy, structure, incentives, benefits, and development that together reward talent.
DART model	The book's frame: Direction and Deployment, Assessment and Attraction, Rewarding and Retaining, and Teaching and Transforming.
Design sequence	The order of operations, strategy through measurement, by which a reward system is built.
The four objectives	Efficiency, fairness, ethics, and compliance, the goals a system must balance.
Defensibility	The quality of a pay decision that can be justified by theory, evidence, and law.
The three tests	Alignment, differentiation, and value, applied to judge a compensation strategy.
Coherence	The fit among a system's parts, so that structure, market posture, incentives, and development point the same way.

Discussion Questions

1. Return to the opening case. Sketch a systemic response to the LAUSD cycle that draws on at least five different chapters of this book.
2. Why does incoherence, rather than any single bad choice, most often break a reward system?
3. Choose two of the four objectives (efficiency, fairness, ethics, compliance) and describe a real trade-off between them and how you would resolve it.
4. What makes a pay decision defensible in California specifically, and how is that different from defensibility elsewhere?
5. Compare the LAUSD and FAA cases. What does each teach about designing whole systems rather than fragments?

Capstone Case · Design a Compensation System

Choose a real California organization (public, private, or nonprofit) that you know or can research. Using the design sequence and the DART model, build a compensation approach for it: state its strategy and pay philosophy, map the California legal requirements it faces, describe how it should value and price its jobs, propose a base structure and where it should lead, lag, or match, decide whether and where incentives fit, outline a benefits and total-rewards approach, and name the metrics by which it would judge success.

Capstone requirements

1. Tie every major choice to one of the book's frameworks (DART, the pay model, the four-step process, or the three tests).
2. Name at least one real trade-off among efficiency, fairness, ethics, and compliance, and defend your resolution.
3. Identify the California legal requirements that constrain or shape your design.
4. Specify how you would measure, after one year, whether the system worked, and how you would defend it to a skeptical board.

Capstone Case · Aptus Group, an Educational-Staffing Firm

Aptus Group is a real California company that puts every chapter of this book to work at once. Founded in 2008 and led by chief executive Cinthya Vodanovich, Aptus provides educational-staffing services to school districts across Southern California. It has grown to more than fifty employees and over a million dollars in annual services, with roughly fourteen in-house staff, in recruiting, client relations, accounting, and consulting, supporting about forty-five billable employees, credentialed educators and aspiring teachers, placed across twenty-five districts.

Aptus faces the classic problems of a people business. It must reduce the time it takes to hire and place qualified educators without lowering quality; keep placed employees engaged and loyal even though they work at client sites rather than at Aptus; and grow at a pace it can sustain and afford. Its product is its people, so its compensation system is not a back-office function; it is the business model.

Capstone task. Acting as a compensation consultant to Aptus, design a complete reward system, for both the in-house team and the billable educators, and defend it. Work through the design sequence and tie each choice to the book's frameworks.

Case questions

1. Apply the DART model to Aptus. What does Direction and Deployment look like when half the workforce sits at client sites, and where do Assessment and Attraction, Rewarding and Retaining, and Teaching and Transforming each bear on the firm's stated problems?
2. Design base pay for two very different populations, the in-house staff and the billable educators, using internal alignment, market pricing, and a defensible structure. Where would you lead, match, or lag, and why?
3. Engagement of placed workers is a named pain point. Which non-cash and relational rewards would you use to keep employees loyal to Aptus when they spend their days inside another organization?
4. Identify the California legal requirements that shape the design, from wage-and-hour and pay transparency to the rules governing staffing and contract labor.
5. Specify the few metrics you would track to know, a year later, whether the system reduced time-to-hire, improved engagement, and supported sustainable growth, and how you would defend it to Aptus's leadership.

References

ABC7 Los Angeles. (2023). *LAUSD, teachers union reach tentative labor agreement*; and coverage of the 2023 LAPD contract. https://abc7.com/lausd-teachers-union-labor-agreement-utla/13149284/

Brown, B. (2015). Rising strong: How the ability to reset transforms the way we live, love, parent, and lead. Spiegel & Grau.

Federal Aviation Administration. (2025). *Air traffic controller workforce plan 2025-2028.* https://www.faa.gov/about/office_org/headquarters_offices/afn/offices/finance/offices/office-financial-labor-analysis/plans/controller-workforce.pdf

Milkovich, G. T., Newman, J. M., & Gerhart, B. (2023). *Compensation* (14th ed.). McGraw-Hill Education.

Sinek, S. (2019). The infinite game. Portfolio.

About the Author

Thomas J. Norman, Ph.D., is a professor of management and the author of this book. His teaching and scholarship sit at the intersection of compensation, strategic human resource management, and the changing employment relationship, and they share a single throughline: organizations succeed when they direct, attract, reward, and develop talent as one connected system rather than a set of disconnected programs.

He earned his A.B. in social studies, with a concentration in international relations, from Harvard University, and his M.A. and Ph.D. in human resources and industrial relations from the University of Minnesota. Before becoming a professor, he spent his early career in industry, holding management positions at Procter & Gamble, Sun Microsystems, U.S. Bancorp, Wells Fargo, and Cargill. At Sun Microsystems he managed a global employee-survey program that reached more than 30,000 employees each quarter, served on a team that re-engineered the company's human resources function, and redesigned sales compensation in ways that helped the firm attract talent from far larger competitors. That practitioner experience still anchors his teaching: he reaches for real cases and concrete numbers before theory, and he treats compensation as a tool managers actually have to use.

Dr. Norman's research examines how globalization reshapes the employment relationship, with particular attention to the hidden costs of outsourcing and offshoring, the link between human resource systems and organizational performance, and how reward decisions are made and judged as fair. His published work spans peer-reviewed journals and case studies. An award-winning instructor, he was named his university's Outstanding Professor for excellence in teaching, research, and service, and in 2025 his university president nominated him for the California State University's Wang Family Excellence Award.

His organizing framework for reward strategy, the DART model (Direction and Deployment, Assessment and Attraction, Rewarding and Retaining, and Teaching and Transforming of talent), gives students and managers a shared language for connecting pay to performance. He has mentored more than twenty students into doctoral programs, founded a campus innovation incubator, helped build business and public-administration programs at universities in Ethiopia, Cameroon, Bulgaria, and Albania, and delivered more than seventy invited lectures across China. He also keeps an active executive-coaching practice, advising leaders and founders. He lives in greater Los Angeles.

Glossary

Key terms from across the twelve chapters, in alphabetical order.

Agency problem. The difficulty that arises because owners cannot fully observe agents' actions, addressed partly through incentive design.

Agency theory. The view that owners must design pay so agents' self-interest aligns with the owners' interests.

Aging (trending) data. Adjusting survey data forward to the date the pay will take effect.

Agricultural overtime (AB 1066). California's phased rule, fully effective in 2025, requiring farm employers of all sizes to pay overtime after 8 hours a day or 40 a week.

Alignment test. Does the strategy fit the mission and the rest of the organization's strategy?

AMO. Performance as the product of Ability, Motivation, and Opportunity; any one at zero yields zero.

Benchmark job. A common, stable, well-understood job that appears in most surveys and anchors market pricing.

Benefits. Indirect, largely noncash compensation such as health coverage, retirement, and paid leave.

Best fit. Designing pay for an organization's own strategy, workforce, context, and mission.

Best practices. Designing pay by copying what successful organizations do; best for the technical basics.

Bonus. A one-time performance payout that does not raise base pay.

Broadbanding. Collapsing many narrow grades into a few wide bands for flexibility.

California Equal Pay Act. Labor Code section 1197.5, requiring equal pay for substantially similar work and limiting the defenses an employer may raise.

CalSavers. California's state-run retirement program for employers without a qualified plan.

CFRs (Conversations, Feedback, Recognition). Doerr's pairing for OKRs: ongoing conversations between manager and contributor, mutual specific feedback, and real-time recognition; intended to replace the annual performance review.

Coaching and mentoring. Development that transfers judgment and skill through guided relationships.

Coherence. The fit among a system's parts, so that structure, market posture, incentives, and development point the same way.

Compa-ratio. Employee pay divided by the range midpoint; 1.0 means at the market reference.

Compa-ratio distribution. The spread of employees' compa-ratios, showing whether pay sits sensibly in ranges.

Compensation. The pay employees receive directly and indirectly through wages, salaries, incentives, and benefits.

Compensation dashboard. A regular summary of key reward metrics used to drive decisions.

Compensation objectives. Efficiency, fairness, ethics, and compliance.

Compensation strategy. A coherent set of pay decisions that supports how an organization competes and wins.

Compensation system. The integrated set of strategy, structure, incentives, benefits, and development that together reward talent.

Cost of turnover. The full cost of replacing an employee, used to value retention.

Criteria (job- vs. person-based). The basis for setting levels: the job a person holds (job-based) or the skills and competencies a person brings (person-based).

Current ability. What an employee can do now, the basis for some selection decisions.

DART model. Thomas J. Norman's organizing framework: Direction and Deployment, Assessment and Attraction, Rewarding and Retaining, and Teaching and Transforming of talent.

Defensibility. The quality of a pay decision that can be justified by theory, evidence, and law.

Derived demand. The principle that labor is demanded only because of the value its output creates for employers or the public.

Design sequence. The order of operations, strategy through measurement, by which a reward system is built.

Differentials. The size of the pay gaps between adjacent levels in a structure.

Differentiation test. Does the approach distinguish the organization where distinction matters?

Distributive justice. Perceived fairness of pay outcomes, the actual numbers.

Egalitarian structure. A structure with few levels and small differentials that favors cooperation and interdependent work.

Employee experience. How employees perceive their work, rewards, and treatment over time.

Employment Training Panel (ETP). A California program that co-funds approved employer training to retain skilled workers.

Equity compensation. Stock-based pay (such as RSUs or options) that ties employees to long-run firm value; in private firms it may stay illiquid until a liquidity event.

Equity theory. The view that people compare their contribution-to-reward ratio with others' and act to restore balance when it feels unfair (Adams, 1965).

Exempt employee. An employee who meets a duties test and a salary threshold ($70,304 in California in 2026) and is therefore exempt from overtime.

Existential flexibility. Sinek's term for the willingness to make a major strategic change when the conditions that produced the original strategy have shifted.

Expectancy theory. The view that effort depends on believing effort yields performance, performance yields reward, and the reward is valued.

External competitiveness. How an organization's pay compares with relevant labor markets.

Future ability. What an employee could do after development, the basis for selecting on potential.

Gainsharing. A team incentive that shares the gains from improved productivity or cost savings.

Gaming. Manipulating a metric to earn a reward without producing the intended result.

General Schedule (GS). The U.S. federal pay system of 15 grades and 10 steps per grade.

Green-circle rate. Pay below the range minimum, usually raised on a planned schedule.

Grit. Duckworth's term for passion and perseverance for very long-term goals; predicts outcomes that raw measured ability alone does not.

Hierarchical structure. A structure with many levels and large differentials that favors individual achievement and measurable work.

HP Way. Hewlett-Packard's trust-based management culture (management by walking around, profit sharing, employee security treated as mutual obligation) that migrated to Sun, Apple, Cisco, and other Silicon Valley firms in the late twentieth century.

Human capital theory. The view that pay reflects the value of, and investment in, a person's skills and knowledge.

Hygiene factor. A condition (such as pay) whose absence causes dissatisfaction but whose presence does not strongly motivate.

Iceberg compensation. A teaching visual for total rewards: salary above the waterline, the larger value below (deferred compensation, benefits, retirement, equity).

Incentive function. Compensation's effect on what employees do once on the payroll.

Incentive pay. Pay made contingent on results or performance.

Individual incentive. A reward tied to one person's results (commission, piece rate, individual bonus).

Institutional theory. The view that organizations adopt structures by imitating what is normal in their field (DiMaggio & Powell, 1983).

Interactional justice. Perceived fairness in how pay decisions are communicated: honest explanations and respectful, dignified treatment.

Internal alignment. The consistency of pay relationships across jobs inside the organization.

Internal alignment (internal equity). The pay relationships among the jobs, skills, and competencies within a single organization.

Internal labor market. The system of entry points and promotion ladders by which an organization fills and advances jobs from within.

Just Cause. Sinek's term for an organization's vision of the future that the work serves — the "why" that gives the work meaning beyond the immediate task.

Lead / lag / match. Paying above, below, or at market, chosen role by role.

Legally required benefits. Benefits mandated by law (Social Security, Medicare, unemployment, workers' compensation, and in California SDI and PFL).

Levels. The number of rungs, grades, or bands in a pay structure.

Line of sight. The clarity with which an employee can see how their effort affects their pay.

Market pay line. A line summarizing what the market pays as job value rises.

Market pricing. Matching benchmark jobs to survey data and slotting other jobs relative to the resulting market line.

Merit pay. A performance-based increase folded into base salary.

Midpoint. The market reference point of a range, the intended pay for a fully competent performer.

Minimum wage. The lowest hourly wage an employer may pay; in California, $16.90 statewide in 2026, with higher local and industry rates.

Motivator. A factor (such as recognition, achievement, or growth) that actively drives engagement.

Offer-acceptance rate. The share of job offers candidates accept, a signal of market position.

OKR (Objective and Key Results). Doerr's goal-setting framework: an Objective states what success looks like; three to five Key Results state how anyone will know. The four "superpowers" are Focus, Align, Track, and Stretch.

Organizational incentive. A reward tied to enterprise results (profit sharing, employee stock ownership).

Paid Family Leave (PFL). California benefit providing partial wage replacement to care for family or bond with a new child.

Pay compression. The shrinking of the gap between experienced employees and newcomers until experience is barely rewarded.

Pay data reporting. The annual report of pay and demographics that employers with 100+ employees must file with the California Civil Rights Department.

Pay for performance. Linking reward to measured results so that pay rises and falls with performance.

Pay grade. A group of jobs of roughly equal value, paid and managed as a set.

Pay inversion. The condition in which new hires earn more than more experienced incumbents.

Pay model. The toolkit of objectives, policy choices, and techniques used to design and judge a compensation system.

Pay range. The minimum, midpoint, and maximum pay for a grade.

Pay structure. The array of pay levels and differentials an organization uses to relate its jobs to one another.

Pay transparency. The practice or legal requirement of disclosing compensation information, such as pay ranges.

Pay transparency (SB 1162). California's requirement that employers with 15+ employees post pay scales and disclose them to employees on request.

Pay-equity audit. A structured analysis of whether similar work is paid similarly across groups.

PEPRA. The Public Employees' Pension Reform Act of 2013, which established a lower-tier benefit structure for California public employees hired on or after January 1, 2013, and required them to share half of the normal cost of their pension benefits.

Percentile. A position in the market distribution; the 50th is the median, used to define match, lead, and lag.

Policy choices. Internal alignment, external competitiveness, employee contributions, and management.

Prevailing wage. A legally required wage rate for each craft on public-works projects, set by the Department of Industrial Relations.

Procedural justice. Perceived fairness of the process used to set pay.

Range penetration. How far an employee's pay has moved through the range: (pay - minimum) / (maximum - minimum).

Range spread. The distance from a range's minimum to its maximum, usually wider in higher grades.

Real-time market data. Current labor signals, such as live job-posting ranges, offer-acceptance rates, and time-to-fill, used alongside surveys to track fast-moving skills.

Reassessment. The scheduled review that closes the strategy loop and keeps the system current.

Reckoning, Rumble, Revolution. Brown's three-phase post-mortem framework: name what was felt about the failure (reckoning), interrogate the story being told about why it happened (rumble), then design the next move (revolution).

Recognition. Timely, specific acknowledgment of good work; a low-cost motivator distinct from pay.

Red-circle rate. Pay above the range maximum, usually frozen until the range catches up.

Regretted turnover. Departures of employees the organization wanted to keep.

Relational returns. The non-financial value of work: recognition, status, security, challenge, growth, colleagues, and mission.

Relevant labor market. The set of employers, defined by occupation, industry, geography, and size, that actually compete for a role.

Residual. A payment to writers, actors, and others each time a film or show is reused, rerun, or streamed, so pay continues after the work is done.

Retention. The ability to keep employees, especially those whose departure would reduce performance or raise replacement costs.

Risk pooling. Spreading the cost of uncertain events across many people so no one is ruined by bad luck.

Salary survey. An organized collection of pay data for defined jobs in a defined market.

Salary-history ban. Labor Code section 432.3, which prohibits asking applicants about their pay history.

Sectoral minimum wage. An industry-specific floor above the statewide minimum, such as the fast-food (AB 1228) and health-care (SB 525) rates.

Skill-based pay. Pay tied to the skills and competencies an employee acquires and demonstrates.

Skills premium. A deliberate pay add-on above a role's market line for a scarce or emerging skill, governed by written guardrails and an approval process.

Skills-based pay. Basing pay on the specific, market-valued capabilities a person holds rather than on job title alone.

Sorting function. Compensation's effect on who applies, accepts, and stays.

Stack ranking. A performance-management system that requires managers to allocate employees into a forced distribution of high, middle, and low performers, regardless of absolute performance; canonical at Microsoft from 1996 to 2013.

State Disability Insurance (SDI). California program providing partial wage replacement for non-work disabilities, employee-funded.

Stay interview. A conversation with a current employee about what would keep them, conducted before they consider leaving.

Step system. Many narrow grades, each with fixed steps and rule-based advancement (e.g., the federal General Schedule).

Strengths-based development. Buckingham and Clifton's framework that concentrates developmental investment on an employee's signature strengths rather than on closing weakness gaps.

Stretch assignment. A challenging task or role used to grow capability through real work.

Structure adjustment. Shifting the whole set of ranges upward as the market rises.

Teaching and Transforming Talent. The DART dimension capturing an organization's capacity to grow employee capability over time.

Team incentive. A reward tied to group results (gainsharing, group goal bonus).

The four objectives. Efficiency, fairness, ethics, and compliance, the goals a system must balance.

The three tests. Alignment, differentiation, and value, applied to judge a compensation strategy.

Time-to-fill. How long a vacancy stays open, a signal of competitiveness.

Total compensation. Cash (base, merit, incentives, cost-of-living) plus benefits plus relational returns.

Total rewards. The full value of employment: cash, benefits, and relational returns.

Tournament theory. The view that large differentials near the top act as prizes that intensify competition for promotion (Lazear & Rosen, 1981).

Tuition reimbursement. An employer benefit that funds employee education, linking development to reward.

Turnover cost. The full cost of losing an employee: recruiting, onboarding, lost productivity, and lost knowledge.

Value test. Does the result justify the cost (turnover, productivity, compliance)?

Vicious / virtuous circle. A self-reinforcing cycle that compensation design can worsen or break.

Voluntary benefits. Benefits an employer chooses to offer to compete for talent.

Wage theft. The unlawful denial of earned wages, such as unpaid hours, overtime, or breaks.

Index

Page numbers refer to where each topic is discussed. To populate or refresh, select all (Ctrl+A) and press F9 in Word.

Index by Chapter

A quick reference: each term and the chapter(s) in which it appears.

www.ingramcontent.com/pod-product-compliance
Lightning Source LLC
LaVergne TN
LVHW060037210926
848481LV00013B/3884
9798996378128